UNDERSTANDING
the
END TIMES

*Are Current Events Pointing To
a Soon Return of Jesus?*

RICH CHASSE

WESTBOW
PRESS®
A DIVISION OF THOMAS NELSON
& ZONDERVAN

WestBow Press books may be ordered through booksellers or by contacting:

WestBow Press
A Division of Thomas Nelson & Zondervan
1663 Liberty Drive
Bloomington, IN 47403
www.westbowpress.com
844-714-3454

ISBN: 978-1-6642-7666-6 (sc)
ISBN: 978-1-6642-7667-3 (hc)
ISBN: 978-1-6642-7665-9 (e)

Library of Congress Control Number: 2022916083

Print information available on the last page.

WestBow Press rev. date: 09/02/2022

CONTENTS

SECTIONS 4: FROM THE PERSPECTIVE
OF REVELATION

SECTIONS 5: THE END OF THE STORY

DEDICATION

This book is a labor of love that would not have been possible without the love and support that my family provides. My wife, Sherie, has been a tremendous partner to me for over thirty-five years. She has encouraged me every step of the way in this project. I am honored to be her husband, and I love her more dearly with each passing year. My three children—Sara (with her husband, Ryan), Emma (with her husband, Joshua), and Lucien Davis—have also been sources of encouragement and support to me. They unconditionally love me despite all my impassioned "takes" and opinions on current events. And I love them more than words can express.

My church family has also been a source of encouragement and support. Because we do not live near our birth families, our church, CrossRoads Church of Mason County, Michigan, has been our family for over twenty-two years. Saying, "Thank you," doesn't seem to be enough. Tom Noteware has been my partner in ministry for most of those years, and I cannot imagine my life and work without his faithful service and friendship. We love you all! Sherie and I look forward to serving alongside you in the future.

My mother, Rita Chasse, has also been a great source of love and assurance to me. She has been an example of grace and perseverance for the fifty-eight years of my life, and her continued love and care for her children are inspiring.

Also to my father, Lucien Chasse. When we were both new Christians, we loved to talk about and imagine how all the events of the End Times would come to pass. I miss my Dad and those conversations! I take comfort in knowing that my Dad has been with the Lord Jesus since Christmas 1993. It brings a smile to my face thinking that he has all the answers now. Meanwhile, I'm still here on earth, trying to understand how all these things are going to work out. I look forward to Dad providing a tour of Heaven for me, right after I spend some quality time worshipping Jesus. We'll be together again soon!

Rich Chasse

ACKNOWLEDGMENTS

Early on after becoming a Christian, God called me to serve Him in a way that was different from the direction my life was headed. I was planning to major in nuclear engineering in college. After attending freshman orientation for that program, I realized that the Lord was changing my heart and direction. Through God's providence, I became a student at Cedarville College (now Cedarville University) in Cedarville, Ohio. My major was in the pre-seminary Bible program. It was there that I solidified my understanding of Dispensational Theology and grew in my desire to understand prophecy. This desire was furthered in my time at Dallas Theological Seminary in Dallas, Texas. While I did not finish my degree there, I loved the classes, the rigorous learning, the challenging discussion, and the books. Most important, my time spent studying God's Word and preparing sermons for our congregation has furthered my love for the inspiration, infallibility, and sufficiency of the Scriptures and a clearer understanding of prophecy. I am grateful to both institutions of higher learning I attended and to the local churches I have served in my time since.

I wish to also acknowledge Cheryl Lopatka and Tom Noteware for their invaluable service in the editing of this book. Their work has made this project much better for what they added to the final manuscript. Thank you for taking the time to contribute to this work!

INTRODUCTION

Here we are, another book on the End Times. Will this one be any different from much of the fare we see on the market today? Let's start with what you won't find in this book. You won't find an unnecessary use of sensationalism. Many preachers and authors try to tantalize potential listeners and readers with sensational headlines about current events pointing to a "for certain" soon return of Christ. It might be about how prophecy warns of a pandemic as a sign that the Rapture may happen in a matter of months. Or how a conflict that erupts somewhere in the Middle East points to a potential harbinger of the return of Christ. Or it might be how a rising world leader could perhaps be the future Antichrist of the Tribulation. Or how the color of the moon provides some sort of clue as to the return of Christ. These kinds of statements are an abuse of the biblical view of the events surrounding the Second Coming of Christ. You won't find those tactics used here.

This book presents a traditional Dispensational viewpoint of the End Times. We mention it here to let readers understand our viewpoint in presenting this study of the End Times. Now, you don't have to know what that term means; I permit you to skip this part of the chapter if this confuses you. Just know that this is a time-tested view and holds to a high view of the Scriptures. For example, God made a promise to Israel through King David in 2 Samuel 7:16: "Your house and your kingdom will endure forever before me; your throne will be established forever." We believe that God will fulfill that promise to Israel at the end of the Tribulation in the Millennial Kingdom. There are some who believe that the Church has taken the place of Israel in God's design and that God's promises to Israel will be fulfilled through the Church (Covenant Theology). But Dispensationalists believe that if God promised it to Israel, He will fulfill it *to Israel*. This is, admittedly, a simplistic presentation of the viewpoints. While this book's purpose is not to make the argument for Dispensational Theology against Covenant Theology, we nevertheless stipulate there is much to be gleaned from both viewpoints.

As you make your way through this book, you will notice just how much the Scriptures are used to help us understand End Times events and timelines. This author believes the Scriptures hold the answers, therefore to the Scriptures we will go in the study of the End Times. In the process, we focus on the places in the prophetic literature of both Old and New Testament passages that are presented with clarity and certainty. We won't take the time or space to speculate much on those portions of Scripture where it is more difficult to be certain or dogmatic. For instance, we won't speculate on whether the locusts in Revelation 9 are literal insects or whether they represent military helicopters or something else. Most of the time, the answers to these kinds of passages are just speculation and guesses. On the other hand, when a phrase like, "the thousand years," is used in Revelation 20, it is something that can more likely be understood in a literal sense because of how it is specific it is, how it is repeated several times, and because of how the context helps us to prefer a literal understanding.

Let's go back to what is <u>not</u> another goal for this project. In this book, I do not intend to take a scholarly or academic approach to the subject of the Second Coming of Christ. First, I am not a scholar; nor do I play one on TV. I do appreciate scholars and experts in the realm of theology and Bible exposition. We need academics and scholars. But that is not the world I live in or serve. I am a local church pastor who hopes to speak to the local church. I want people in the pews, as they pick up this book, to be able to read and understand more clearly the issues surrounding the Second Coming of Christ. There is too much speculation and sensationalism on this subject already available. I believe if the average churchgoing, Bible-reading believer has more confidence in the subject of the Second Coming, the less those other speculative and sensationalized books, websites, and preachers will cause them to be uneasy, or even scare them.

The layout of the book is quite simple. There are five sections with three chapters in each section. Section 1 provides a foundation for understanding End Times events. Sections 2 through 5 tell the story of End Times events in somewhat of a chronological order. Section 4, which covers events from the book of Revelation, is a bit harder to understand from a chronological perspective. We'll address the issue of timing in Revelation in chapter 11. Section 5 addresses the events at the very end of the Bible (Revelation 19–22). The last chapter deals with points of application. I believe that just knowing information is not enough. We must apply what we learn to how we live our lives.

My goal for this book is to make much of Jesus Christ. The reason for studying this subject is to have a better understanding of our Savior. Armed with a better understanding of Jesus allows us to be more effective in the ways we live and serve Him. Our devotion to Christ will only continue to grow. The compassion we have for those who don't know Jesus will also continue to grow. The bottom line: All of this is for Jesus.

> Blessed is the one who reads aloud the words of this prophecy, and blessed are those who hear it and take to heart what is written in it, because the time is near. (Revelation 1:3)

I encourage you to begin by reading through the "Glossary of End Times Terms," which follows. This will be time well spent so that you and I can be on the same page in understanding some basic terms and ideas presented in prophetic literature. Are you ready? This is a fascinating subject. You might want to buckle your seat belt. The ride might get a little bumpy, but it will be worth it!

GLOSSARY OF END TIMES TERMS

You might be thinking, *Doesn't a glossary usually go at the back of the book?* That is usually correct. But because many of the terms used when discussing the End Times are loaded with preconceived ideas and are sometimes misunderstood, I thought it best to go through several of the familiar terms and explain them ahead of time, so we'd all be on the same page as we make our way through this study. These terms are listed in the chronological order of when each event will happen. Here we go.

The Rapture: That specific event at the end of the Church Age but before the Tribulation, when all Christians will be "caught up" (from the Latin—*rapturo*) together in the clouds to meet the Lord Jesus in the air. This applies to both the dead in Christ of the Church Age, whose bodies will be instantly resurrected in that moment, and the living in Christ, whose living bodies will be instantly translated into immortal, resurrected bodies. The unbelieving world will not be a witness to this event.

> For the Lord himself will come down from heaven, with a loud command, with the voice of the archangel and with the trumpet call of God, and the dead in Christ will rise first. After that, we who are still alive and are left will be *caught up* together with them in the clouds to meet the Lord in the air. (1 Thessalonians 4:16–17; italics added)

Other rapture-like events will happen at the end of the Tribulation and at the end of the Millennial Kingdom. These events can lead to confusion. For example, Matthew 24:37–41 seems to be addressing the subject of the Rapture, but it is actually speaking of the judgment of the lost at the end of the Tribulation. The key to understanding the passage is in its own context, as Jesus said, "as it was in the days of Noah," which helps us to understand that He was speaking about those who would be "taken away" for judgment, with those left behind being faithful believers who would enter the Kingdom that was upon them. There will be more of an explanation of this in section 1.

The Judgment Seat of Christ: This judgment is reserved for Christians who were part of the Church Age. This will be a judgment, not for sin, but for faithfulness in serving the Lord during a person's lifetime. Reward will be given for faithfulness; unfaithfulness, expressed in improper motives, wrong attitudes, misaligned priorities, or just plain laziness, will result in loss of reward. This judgment will take place after the Rapture of the Church.

The Marriage Supper of the Lamb: This grand celebration will take place after the Rapture and the Judgment Seat of Christ and before the actual Second Coming of Christ. This celebration will only include Church Age saints from the beginning of the Church after the resurrection of Jesus to the end of the Church Age with the Rapture. Remember, the Church is the Bride of Christ, therefore it is fitting this would be a celebration that would only include the Church.

The Tribulation: This is the seven-year period after the Church is raptured or taken up out of the earth, and God will again be dealing with Israel, bringing judgment upon Israel and the whole earth for its rejection of Jesus as the Messiah. God will also use this time, particularly at the end of the Tribulation, to fulfill the promises He made to the nation of Israel to Abraham, Moses, and David.

The Gospel of the Kingdom: This is the specific gospel message that John the Baptist and Jesus proclaimed during their ministries on the earth. The specific message was, "The kingdom of God has come near. Repent and believe the good news!" (Mark 1:15). This is the gospel message that will also be proclaimed during the Tribulation (Matthew 24:14). But it is not the message we are proclaiming today. For us in the Church Age, the Kingdom of God is *not* near, not in the same way it was when Jesus was offering the Kingdom during His earthly ministry, or the way it will literally be near or at hand during the

Tribulation. The message we are proclaiming today is, as Paul declared to the Ephesian elders,

> However, I consider my life worth nothing to me; my only aim is to finish the race and complete the task the Lord Jesus has given me—the task of testifying to *the good news of God's grace.* (Acts 20:24; italics added)

It is the "good news of God's grace" that we are proclaiming today. The Kingdom is not being offered to us *today.* Knowing this distinction helps us to understand some of the more difficult to interpret passages in the four Gospels. This may sound different from what you have heard before, but let the text of Scripture speak for itself.

The Antichrist: It is during the Tribulation that the man identified as the Antichrist will rise to power promising peace, but in the end proves his evil intentions by proclaiming that he must be worshipped instead of the Lord Jesus Christ. In the end, the Antichrist will meet his doom and be sent to eternal damnation.

The Abomination of Desolation: This is a specific event that will occur at the midway point of the seven-year Tribulation (at the three-and-a-half-year point). The Antichrist will rise to enter the Temple in Jerusalem, declare himself to be (G)od, and demand to be worshipped. As he does this, millions of people, particularly Jews, will recognize that the Antichrist is, in fact, not God but the devil. They will have to flee or be slaughtered by the Antichrist, who will have consolidated all the world's powers, along with their armies, under his control.

The Second Coming of Christ: There are two ways to understand the concept that is known as the Second Coming of Christ. The first is the specific event that will occur at the end of the Tribulation. This is when Jesus will very literally and very loudly return to the earth to execute His judgment and wrath upon the devil and his kind, upon the enemies of the Lord, and upon those who hate the Lord's people. This is in stark contrast to the Rapture, which will only be witnessed by those who are believers in Christ and occurs before the beginning of the Tribulation.

But there are also times when the Second Coming of Christ refers to the whole of End Times events, including the Rapture, the

Tribulation, the actual Second Coming, and the beginning of the Millennial Kingdom.

The Day of the Lord, or "that Day": This phrase is used throughout both the Old and New Testaments. Like the Second Coming, it can have two meanings. One is about the specific day that Jesus returns to judge the world and usher in His Kingdom (the Millennial Kingdom). But it can also refer to all the End Times events together. As you read each passage of Scripture, you will need to understand each one's context to determine if it is a reference to the former or the latter.

The Millennial Kingdom: This is the literal one-thousand-year rule of Jesus Christ on the earth that will take place after the Tribulation. It is spoken of in both the Old and New Testaments. Those who are saints from both the Old Testament era and the Church Age will reign with Christ in resurrected bodies during this time. Old Testament saints will be resurrected at the beginning of the Millennial Kingdom, as well as those who are martyred during the Tribulation. The saints who survive the time of the Tribulation will go into the Millennial Kingdom with their regular bodies and will marry and have children and families during this thousand-year period.

The Great White Throne Judgment: This judgment will take place after the Millennial Kingdom. It will include all the lost people from all ages—whether during Old Testament time, New Testament, or during the Tribulation. All the lost will be judged at this time. To put it simply, if you are a Christian, you will not be involved with this judgment.

We will come across more terms, and we will explain them as they occur in our study.

SECTION 1

LAYING THE GROUNDWORK

CHAPTER 1

HACKING THROUGH
THE DEEP WEEDS

Pᴇᴏᴘʟᴇ ᴀʀᴇ ꜰᴀsᴄɪɴᴀᴛᴇᴅ ᴀɴᴅ sᴏᴍᴇᴛɪᴍᴇs terrified by the subject of the End Times and the book of Revelation. It can be disturbing; for some people, it can be scary. There's a lot of misinformation out there. Many false teachers are playing on the insecurities of many people with so-called End Times updates that stir up fear or curiosity, taking advantage of many as a result. In this book, we attempt to hack through the deep weeds of what is currently available in this kind of literature. We'll spend most of our time in the New Testament, but we'll also look at some passages from the Old Testament. When we get on the other side of these deep weeds and into the clearing, my prayer, my hope, and my goal are that we have a renewed sense of hope and a feeling of confidence about what is to come.

But we're not going to pretend that we know all the answers. It's not appropriate to say that we understand every detail or have everything figured out concerning the things that are to come. That's not our goal. That's not the purpose of what we're doing. It is instead to point to Jesus and to understand that He is the one who gives us that sense of hope and that feeling of confidence in all this.

To get things going, we need to answer a big question. We're going to delve into some principles of Bible study that are useful, not just for prophetic literature and understanding prophecy, but for understanding all the Scriptures. And we're going to kick things off with some passages of Scripture that deal with End Times and the Second Coming of Christ prophecy. Let's start in Matthew 24 and Luke 21:

> Jesus answered: "Watch out that no one deceives you. For many will come in my name, claiming, 'I am the Messiah,' and will deceive many. You will hear of wars and rumors of wars, but see to it that you are not alarmed. Such things must happen, but the end is still to come. Nation will rise against nation, and kingdom against kingdom. There will be famines and earthquakes in various places. All these are the beginning of birth pains." (Matthew 24:4–8)

> There will be great earthquakes, famines and pestilences in various places, and fearful events and great signs from heaven. (Luke 21:11)

Jesus is speaking in these parallel passages, answering a question from the disciples about the "sign" of His Second Coming. He said there would be terrifying things and great miraculous signs from heaven. Jesus said that all these things would be, "the beginning of birth pains." Any of you moms might remember the beginnings of birth pains. Thankfully, I didn't get to experience birth pains. The subject of labor pains comes up again in another passage, this time from the apostle Paul, who didn't write much prophetic literature. But he did write a few things in 1 and 2 Thessalonians:

> Now, brothers and sisters, about times and dates we do not need to write to you, for you know very well that the day of the Lord will come like a thief in the night. While people are saying, "Peace and safety," destruction will come on them suddenly, as labor pains on a pregnant woman, and they will not escape. (1 Thessalonians 5:1–3)

If you've been a Christian for several decades, you may remember the seventies. We might need a VH1 episode on the seventies to remember what that decade was like. Back then there was a movie called *Thief in the Night* and then several sequels that terrified youth groups for two decades or so. Or maybe you recall the *Left Behind* series of books and movies. We don't show those anymore, but the stories in them were somewhat based on Scripture.

So here is our big question based on these passages of Scripture:

Are current events pointing to a soon return of Jesus?

Another way of asking the question is, "Are events happening in these last few years pointing to a soon return of Jesus?" Think of all the things you see happening when you turn on the news, flip through your social media, or see elsewhere on the internet. These last couple years have been a blast, right? Do you sense the sarcasm? Have you had enough of it? And yet again, how do we answer this question? Are current events pointing to a soon return of Jesus?

Let me answer the question. I won't dodge it or dance around it.

The short answer: NO.

Now I'm thinking that some of you are disappointed with my answer. Let me demonstrate why the answer is NO for several reasons. But first, let me ask you this. Has everything that has happened since 2020 proved to be a unique historical period? How would you answer this question? Would you say we are in a unique time in world history?

Again, I would say No.

Are we currently facing unprecedented events in world history?

No, not really.

Now, these last few years—2020 and following—do seem kind of bad to me. But let's do a little bit of a comparison, shall we? That period might seem bad, but let's talk about some of the things that we just read in Matthew 24, Luke 21, and 1 Thessalonians 5. Let us also consider what we find in the book of Revelation. First, let's compare 2020 to 1918, a little over one hundred years ago. Do you remember that period? Let me remind you. Let's go back to our high school world history class (or maybe it was a freshman-level world history class in college) and review what happened around 1918.

Jesus talked about wars and rumors of wars, and certainly, wars are going on right now. As I write this, Russia has attacked its neighbor to the west in Ukraine. The United States has just ended a twenty-year war in Afghanistan. There's a war going on in Yemen, and there was recently a war in Syria. What is happening in Mexico between the drug cartels and the military is war, even though we don't often think of it as such.

Now, can you tell me what kind of wars were going on around 1918? The Great War concluded in 1918. It was called that at the time because of the number of countries involved and the substantial loss of life. The world certainly didn't anticipate there being a second Great War. It didn't become known as World War I until after World War II arrived on the world's doorstep. They thought the Great War was the "war to end all wars." Over eight million people died in World War I, so I think 1918 has got us beat in terms of war.

Here's another angle on the subject of war. In 2020, we had the rise of atheistic Marxism here in the good old United States. We thought that beast had been slain with the end of the USSR. And yet, here it is again. Of course, in 1917, there was the Bolshevik Revolution in Russia, which was the rise of Marxist communism. It led to the Russian Civil War, where another six to seven million people died, mostly civilians, in the years after 1917.

Let's talk about hurricanes. We had two hurricanes in Louisiana in 2020. Cameron Parish in Southwest Louisiana was particularly hard hit. A total of thirty-two people died in those two hurricanes. Well, guess who had a hurricane in 1918? That's right, Cameron Parish in Southwest Louisiana. Thirty-four people lost their lives in that hurricane.

Let's talk about earthquakes, shall we? Several earthquakes occurred worldwide between the years 1918 and 2020. In 1918, there was a total loss of life of 2,219. In 2020, there was a total loss of life of 180. That's a notable decrease. But in Matthew 24, Jesus implied earthquakes would be on the increase.

Now, a few of us might have a bit of experience with a little something called COVID-19, the coronavirus pandemic. As I write, the pandemic is waning, and thus far, there have been a total of six million deaths worldwide. An unknown percentage of those deaths are categorized as being, "death *with* COVID," versus, "death *caused by* COVID." Back in 1918, they had something similar to our COVID-19 pandemic called the Spanish flu, which affected the world in four waves. In other words, there was a wave of the flu, and then it seemed like it would be suppressed for a while. Another wave would hit, and so on. The four waves of this flu killed over fifty million people, which many consider a low estimate.

When talking about famine, there hasn't been much in our media about famines happening today. But because of war or regional battles, there are now articles talking about the coming of famines, particularly in Yemen, South Sudan, and the Democratic Republic of the Congo. In 1918, there was a famine in Persia (modern-day Iran), mostly the result of World War I. That famine killed two million people. Would you agree that the times we're living in now seem almost mild in comparison?

Remember how Paul said people would be talking about peace and safety? In 2020, there were several historic peace agreements in the Middle East between Israel, the United Arab Emirates, and Bahrain. But what was going on in the Middle East in 1918? Actually, there was the little battle of Megiddo, which led to the fall of the Ottoman Empire in 1918. Does Megiddo sound familiar to you? Do you know where Megiddo is? It is, in fact, a valley in Israel. If you are a student of prophecy, both Old Testament and in the book of Revelation, the valley of Megiddo is where the final conflict before the Second Coming of Jesus happens in a battle known as Armageddon. Have you heard of Armageddon? Armageddon is based on the valley of Megiddo.

I can imagine that people in churches in 1918, when they were reading about this battle going on in Megiddo, were scared by the developments. I can imagine them asking, "Is this the end?" I mean, they had the Great War, all these plagues, the Russian Revolution, a battle in the valley of Megiddo that led to the end of the Ottoman Empire, and so much more!

So you have all these events, all these "signs" pointing to the coming of the end. I think it's normal to see all these things and ask, "Are they pointing to the soon return of Jesus?" Could they have asked that in 1918? You bet! And they could have asked it in the thirties and forties with the rise of Adolf Hitler and the Nazis in Germany. And just for fun, back when Hitler came to power, he was thought to be the Antichrist. And then in the eighties, when Mikhail Gorbachev came to power in the USSR, some folks thought he might be the Antichrist. Remember that birthmark on his head? Everybody thought that was the mark of the beast. But no, he wasn't the Antichrist. People were saying that maybe Barack Obama was the Antichrist. Or the pope is the Antichrist. Or Donald Trump is the Antichrist. There were theories and opinions about how different leaders on the world stage were, in one way or another, the Antichrist.

And then you've got 1948, when the headline was about Israel becoming a nation. That was big news because people thought it meant that Jesus was coming! Well, Jesus *is* coming. But that doesn't mean Israel becoming a nation in 1948 meant Jesus was coming right then. The book of Revelation speaks of a two-million-man army that marches toward the Middle East from the East. And then news came out that China's got two million men in their army! The reaction was, "That's prophecy! It's gonna happen!" Okay. Maybe there will be a two-million-man army during the Tribulation, but that doesn't mean it's happening next week.

Articles came out recently about how in Jerusalem, elements of the Old Testament Temple are currently being assembled. These are the necessary articles and furniture that would be in use again for the sacrificial system in the Temple. And if that's going to happen, there must be a rebuilt Temple in Jerusalem, where a mosque currently sits on what is the original Temple mount. And there is a fascination with blood moons and cracking prophetic codes and the implanting of microchips in people's hands. We see all this and ask, "Is it time for Jesus to come back?"

Now, those things will come to pass. But not during the Church Age, the age in which we live. They will happen during the Tribulation. In these next few chapters, we're going to take a clear-eyed, levelheaded approach to prophetic Scripture, and we're going to see what the Bible tells us about the Second Coming of Jesus.

CHAPTER 2

JESUS *IS* COMING AGAIN

Now, make no mistake. The Bible makes this very clear: Jesus is coming again. That much we know is going to happen. As we look at the world stage and these events, we're sometimes reminded of the things found in the book of Revelation or Matthew 24. They're startling! We see these things written on the page in Scripture, and then we see it seemingly happening on the news. But let's not be alarmed. And let's not be alarmists either. Jesus is coming, and we should be prepared for that.

Let's take a look at the beginning of the book of Revelation and talk about what this is all about.

> The revelation from Jesus Christ, which God gave him to show his servants what must soon take place. He made it known by sending his angel to his servant John, who testifies to everything he saw—that is, the word of God and the testimony of Jesus Christ. Blessed is the one who reads aloud the words of this prophecy, and blessed are those who hear it and take to heart what is written in it, because the time is near. (Revelation 1:1–3)

This is the apostle John writing at the end of his life. He's stuck on the island of Patmos all by himself. He has a vision of Jesus, who comes to him. This is not John's revelation at all. This is a revelation from

Jesus that John received and then revealed. It is a revelation *from* Jesus, and it is *about* Jesus. The word "revelation" itself is an interesting one. Revelation means, "a pealing back," "a revealing," and, "an unveiling of something that was hidden." From the Greek word (the New Testament was written in Greek) for "revelation," we get our English word "apocalypse." Have you heard of the apocalypse before? It just means a revealing, an unveiling.

He tells us that what is being revealed are things that "must soon take place." It's interesting to note that in the first century, believers were certain that the events surrounding the Second Coming of Jesus would take place in their lifetimes. Every generation of Christians since then have believed that the return of Jesus would happen in their lifetimes. Was it appropriate for them to believe that? Absolutely! Is it proper for us to believe that Jesus will return in our lifetimes? The answer to that question is also yes.

Notice Revelation 1:3 again: "Blessed is the one who reads aloud the words of this prophecy." You and I are blessed if we read the book of Revelation. When you do read it, there might be some stuff in there that sounds quite alarming. Really. Be aware of that. But still, you will be blessed if you read it and blessed if you hear it and take it to heart. Notice the phrase at the end of the verse. He says, "the time is near," or, "the time is at hand." When we're talking about the events surrounding the Second Coming of Jesus, a key word to remember is "imminent." Imminent means it, "could happen at any time." It is "impending," "it could happen at any moment." Imminent means there is one event we believe that, when it arrives, will kick off all the other events. It means:

> There is nothing more in biblical prophecy that must happen before the Rapture of the Church.

What this means is we are not waiting for some sort of sign from the heavens or some specific event that would somehow signal that Christ will soon return. There is no political event, no war, no pandemic, no earthquake, no hurricane, or no massive abandoning of the faith that must occur before Jesus comes to take the Church to

Heaven. It does us no good to try and look at world events or study the Scriptures in search of the so-called signs of the times. All of Scripture telling us to do so are passages dealing with events *during* the Tribulation, not before. It is not helpful to try and figure out if someone might be the Antichrist because he will not be revealed until after the start of the Tribulation.

The one event we're waiting for that will kick off all the other events is the Rapture of the Church. Nothing else. For example, we're not waiting for Israel to be established as a nation (it happened in 1948) to say, "That's a sign foretelling the Rapture of the Church." That specific event didn't have to happen for the Rapture to occur.

Here's another one. The book of Revelation speaks of a Temple. The book of Daniel also refers to a Temple in the End Times. There is currently no Temple in Jerusalem. So if we see that they're going to rebuild the Temple in Jerusalem, or any hints to that effect, people will say, "That's a sign that the Rapture could happen any day now." No, it's not.

The Temple could be rebuilt today, but the Second Coming of Jesus might not happen for centuries. Yes, the Temple will be rebuilt, but it could be rebuilt during the Tribulation (the seven-year period after the Rapture). There is nothing more in prophecy that must happen on the biblical calendar before the Rapture of the Church, the sudden removal of the New Testament Church believers. That's you and me. In the next section, we examine this event called the Rapture. But for now, those of you who are familiar with the Rapture might look at language like this in Matthew 24 and perhaps be a little confused.

> But about that day or hour no one knows, not even
> the angels in heaven, nor the Son, but only the Father.
> (Matthew 24:36)

This passage of Scripture is *not* about the Rapture. Let me repeat this: It is not about the Rapture. This verse has nothing to do with the Rapture of the Church. It is speaking exclusively, implicitly about the Second Coming of Jesus, a separate event that will take place at the end of the Tribulation. Matthew 24 is exclusively about the events of the Tribulation and the Second Coming of Christ. The Church is not in view at all. This will become clearer when we get to the section concerning Matthew 24.

The same is true for this passage in Luke:

> The master of that servant will come on a day when he does not expect him and at an hour he is not aware of. (Luke 12:46)

Once again, in context, this passage has nothing to do with the Rapture of the Church. When Jesus is speaking like this in Matthew and Luke, He is talking specifically about Tribulation events and the Second Coming of Jesus. As we go through Matthew 24 in the next section, we'll explain how this works and why it ends up being this way. Matthew 24–25 is a well-known passage called the Olivet Discourse. It sounds like a fancy name, but the only reason it's called that is because Jesus was speaking on the Mount of Olives, just outside Jerusalem. It has what would have been a nice view of the city and the Temple area.

Take a look at the chart provided labeled "Timeline of the End Times," with a subhead of "According to Matthew 24–25." I want you to notice that there are no references in Matthew 24–25 concerning the Rapture of the Church. None. We'll explain all of this as we make our way through it. In Matthew 24–25, Jesus is answering a specific question His disciples asked Him: "What will be the sign of your coming and of the end of the age?" What will be the sign that lets us know that the end of the age is near? Notice the context. At the end of chapter 23, Jesus talked about going away. He talked about coming back again, and that upset the disciples greatly because the whole idea of Jesus going away, well, they didn't want to talk about that.

TIMELINE OF THE END TIMES
(ACCORDING TO MATTHEW 24–25)

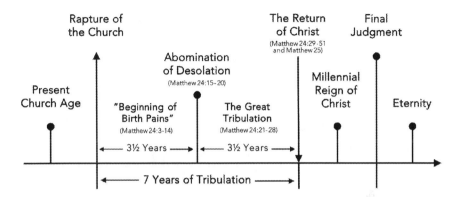

So they asked Jesus, "What will be the sign of your coming and of the end of the age?" What we have in Matthew 24–25 is Jesus answering that very specific question dealing with what's known as the Tribulation, that seven-year period when God is dealing once again with Israel, not the Church. The Church is not in view in Matthew 24–25 at all.

The same is true in the book of Revelation. Once you get past chapter 3 in Revelation, the Church is gone! No more reference to the Church, no more reference to God as Father. In a sense, in Revelation chapters 4–18, the times reflect more of an Old Testament economy or reference point in terms of God beginning to deal with unfinished business He has with Israel, His chosen nation. And yet the Savior, the Messiah, has already come and shed His blood, died, and rose again.

CHAPTER 3

PRECAUTIONS WHEN READING PROPHECY

There are some things to look for when you're reading Bible prophecy—or when reading the Bible period. Some basic principles of interpretation are necessary to understanding Scripture. Especially so for prophetic literature: Matthew 24–25, 1 Thessalonians 4–5, 2 Thessalonians 3, the book of Revelation, the book of Daniel, and several other passages in the Old Testament that are prophetic in nature.

Make Sure to Always Consider the Context of Any Passage

When you pull verses out of context, you're getting into trouble. You're getting into some theological junk. For example, if you pull some passages from Matthew 24, in particular, out of their context and say, "This is talking about the Rapture of the Church," you will end up in some deep weeds trying to understand the timeline of events. We'll look at why in the following chapters.

Don't Make Assumptions about What a Passage Might Mean

There are some verses in Matthew 24, for example, that when viewed, automatically brings to mind the word "rapture."

> As it was in the days of Noah, so it will be at the coming of the Son of Man. For in the days before the flood, people were eating and drinking, marrying and giving in marriage, up to the day Noah entered the ark; and they knew nothing about what would happen until the flood came and took them all away. That is how it will be at the coming of the Son of Man. Two men will be in the field; one will be taken and the other left. Two women will be grinding with a hand mill; one will be taken and the other left. Therefore keep watch, because you do not know on what day your Lord will come. (Matthew 24:37–42)

Jesus is talking here about two men standing in a field. One is taken; one gets left behind. Two women are grinding with a hand mill. One is taken and the other left behind. Immediately, when we see that kind of language, what event do you think of? The Rapture, of course.

But it's not the Rapture! Don't assume it's the Rapture. I'll explain in more detail in the next section. But just because it sounds like the Rapture of the Church, don't assume that's what it's talking about. The key is the context, the phrase just before those seemingly talking about the Rapture. Jesus said the end of the age will be, "as it was in the days of Noah." What happened in the days of Noah? That is key to understanding what Jesus was talking about in the next sentences. So don't make assumptions.

Language and Grammar Matter

When I was a freshman in high school, I studied grammar in English class. And I was a terrible student, which meant that I did terrible in freshmen English grammar. I struggled mightily with diagramming sentences and all that. I got a D– in my freshman year of English. I was bad. (I also flunked algebra.) It was horrible. What's interesting is that the most English grammar I ever learned, particularly diagramming sentences and understanding the use of language, was when I took Greek in college. It may not make much sense, but if I didn't understand the English, I was never going to learn the Greek. I was like a remedial student learning the English language all over again. It was a big deal! Look at this example:

> For the Lord himself will come down from heaven, with a loud command, with the voice of the archangel and with the trumpet call of God, and the dead in Christ will rise first. After that, *we* who are still alive and are left will be caught up together with them in the clouds to meet the Lord in the air. And so *we* will be with the Lord forever. Therefore encourage one another with these words. (1 Thessalonians 4:16–18; italics added)

> Now, brothers and sisters, about times and dates we do not need to write to you, for you know very well that the day of the Lord will come like a thief in the night. While people are saying, "Peace and safety," destruction will come on *them* suddenly, as labor pains on a pregnant woman, and *they* will not escape. (1 Thessalonians 5:1–3; italics added)

Do you remember pronouns from grammar class? Notice the italicized pronouns in both passages. At the end of chapter 4, Paul refers to the people he's writing to as "we." At the beginning of chapter 5, Paul refers to "they" and "them." It matters when you read grammar and language. It helps us to understand the proper interpretation of the passage.

LET THE CLEAR PASSAGES OF SCRIPTURE HELP YOU TO UNDERSTAND THE DIFFICULT ONES

What do you do when you come across a passage of Scripture and think, *Whoa, I have no clue what he's talking about there?* I'm a pastor. I've been a pastor for about three decades. You might think, naively, *He's got the Bible figured out.* But I tell you, there are passages of Scripture that I don't understand. But that's okay. Even the apostle Peter said,

> (Paul's) letters contain some things that are hard to understand, which ignorant and unstable people distort, as they do the other Scriptures, to their own destruction. (2 Peter 3:16)

Now, if one of the original twelve apostles can say, "When I read some of Paul's stuff, I don't get it." I think it's perfectly fine if you and I don't get it either. But we should always remember the clearly stated, easy-to-understand passages of Scripture should always inform us when it comes to interpreting a more difficult-to-understand passage or a difficult-to-apply passage.

Now back to our passage in Revelation chapter 1. John writes to the seven churches in the province of Asia, which is in the southwest of modern-day Turkey (this is not the same as the modern-day continent of Asia):

> "Look, he is coming with the clouds," and "every eye will see him, even those who pierced him"; and all peoples on earth "will mourn because of him." So shall it be! Amen. "I am the Alpha and the Omega," says the Lord God, "who is, and who was, and who is to come, the Almighty." (Revelation 1:7–8)

When you read that first phrase—"Look, he is coming with the clouds"—again you might be tempted to think, *It's the Rapture!* But again, it's not. The clue is the next phrase: "every eye will see him." That won't be true at the Rapture. Only the Church, the believers in Jesus Christ, will see Jesus at the Rapture. And then it says, "even those who pierced him." What is that about? I thought all the people who put Jesus to death, who crucified Him, were long gone, dead. And they are there. But what is that? Notice the footnote. This phrase is a reference to a piece of literature in the Old Testament book of Zechariah, in chapter 12.

> And I will pour out on the house of David and the inhabitants of Jerusalem a spirit of grace and supplication. They will look on me, the one they have pierced, and they will mourn for him as one mourns for an only child, and grieve bitterly for him as one grieves for a firstborn son. (Zechariah 12:10)

To whom is God speaking in this passage? He's talking to the nation of Israel. That's the house of David. The Lord says that they would look on the one they pierced and mourn for Him as one would mourn for an only child. Back in Revelation chapter 1, that is a reference to the nation of Israel mourning, grieving almost in unison, as they come to recognize that they had missed it. They missed that Jesus was their Messiah. This moment will hit them at the middle point of the Tribulation, at an event called the Abomination of Desolation, when the person known as the Antichrist will march up the steps of the Temple and say, "I am God—worship me." And it's as if the veil is removed from the eyes of the nation of Israel. And they will recognize, "We blew it! We crucified Him! We who are Israel, His own people, His namesake; we did this, we crucified Him, we pierced Him!" And they will mourn.

It's at that moment, that Jesus said (this is my paraphrase of Matthew 24:15–21), "You'd better get outta Dodge. Get out of town! You'd better run for your life! Because if you don't, your head is coming off. Literally." Many will lose their lives in that season. Back in Revelation 1:7, the Lord says, "So shall it be! Amen. I am the Alpha and Omega," the beginning and the end. I am the Lord God, "who is, and who was, and who is to come, the Almighty."

This next verse is the theme of our journey together to understand the End Times and the Second Coming of Jesus:

They triumphed over him by the blood of the Lamb
and by the word of their testimony; they did not
love their lives so much as to shrink from death.
(Revelation 12:11)

The "they" is a reference to the Tribulation saints. It's not a reference
to us in the Church Age. These are the people who became followers of
Christ during the difficulties of the Tribulation. They triumphed; they
overcame him, the evil one, literally the dragon or Satan. They overcame
him by the blood of the Lamb and by the word of their testimony.
And they did not love their lives so much as to shrink from death. In
other words, when it became decision time for these believers during
the Tribulation, when confronted with the choice of Jesus and death or
to receive the mark of the beast and follow the new world order, these
believers chose not to shrink from death. They chose Jesus. I am writing
this as if it is history, and that is what prophecy is. It is future history.

SECTION 2

THE RAPTURE AND MORE

CHAPTER 4

UNDERSTANDING THE RAPTURE

THE RAPTURE OF THE CHURCH is not the same as the Second Coming of Jesus. The Second Coming of Jesus refers to the bodily return of Jesus to this planet. But what's known as the Rapture is describing Jesus coming to the clouds to take us (the Church) up and away to Heaven. The Rapture is the event that we refer to as being imminent. It could happen at any moment. It is impending. It could happen five minutes from now. It could happen five hundred years from now. We simply don't know. For those of us living in the Church Age, we are just anticipating, looking forward to the Rapture. One of the main passages of Scripture dealing with the Rapture is found in 1 Thessalonians 4:13–18:

> Brothers and sisters, we do not want you to be uninformed about those who sleep in death, so that you do not grieve like the rest of mankind, who have no hope. For we believe that Jesus died and rose again, and so we believe that God will bring with Jesus those who have fallen asleep in him. According to the Lord's word, we tell you that we who are still alive, who are left until the coming of the Lord, will certainly not precede those who have fallen asleep. For the Lord himself will come down from heaven, with a loud command, with the voice of the archangel and with the trumpet call of God,

and the dead in Christ will rise first. After that, we who are still alive and are left will be caught up together with them in the clouds to meet the Lord in the air. And so we will be with the Lord forever. Therefore encourage one another with these words. (1 Thessalonians 4:13–18)

Paul told them that he didn't want them to be uninformed. The Thessalonian believers were fearful their loved ones who had already died had missed the Second Coming of Christ. Paul was trying to reassure them. He had apparently taught them about the subject when he was with them in person. Either they got mixed up in their heads or they forgot. In his two letters to the Thessalonians, he reminded them of what he previously taught. We don't want to be uninformed about this either. Even though this may be a difficult subject, it's important to try to understand what is to come.

Paul taught them—and us—that we don't have to worry about or grieve those who sleep in death. The rest of humankind has no hope for those who die without Christ. For them, there's nothing to look forward to. But we who are believers in Christ, do have hope. We believe that Jesus died and rose again. It's a part of what it means to be a Christian, that Jesus died on the cross, and then on the third day, He rose from the dead. And then He later ascended to Heaven. As Christians, we believe that we will also be resurrected.

Notice how Paul refers to those who have "fallen asleep" in Christ. He's not talking about people who have taken a nap. He's talking about people who have died. It's similar to the way we talk about someone who has "passed away." When we say someone passed away, we understand what that means. Just like in their context, in their culture, when they talk about someone who had fallen asleep, it was their way of saying someone died. So just like we might have questions about what happens to the people we love when they die, they had doubts and questions and worries about their loved ones who died.

Paul continued, "we tell you that we who are still alive, who are left until the coming of the Lord, will certainly not precede (come before) those who have fallen asleep." Those who had died in Christ, meaning they were Christians, will be the first to be raptured, or caught up to meet the Lord in the air. Paul said that the moment would be introduced with a loud command and a trumpet call. This won't be weak or faint. It will be loud, very loud! What's unique about this loud command and trumpet blast is that the only people who will hear it are believers. Unbelievers won't hear it; the command and trumpet call are not intended for them. It's only intended for the Church.

Paul goes on, "the dead in Christ will rise first." The dead in Christ will be resurrected from the dead first. "After that, we who are still alive and are left will be caught up (there's our word *rapturo*) together with them in the clouds to meet the Lord in the air." We who are still alive and remaining will be raptured, caught up together with them (the dead in Christ who had just been raptured) in the clouds to meet the Lord in the air. A split second later, after the dead in Christ are raptured, those of us who are alive at that moment will be caught up to meet the Lord as well. Our bodies will be instantly changed. You might even say resurrected. In that moment, our bodies will go from mortal to immortal, from corruptible to incorruptible, from perishable to imperishable. "And so we will be with the Lord forever." But the story is not over. What a promise! That is truly something to look forward to.

Please understand your loved ones who have died are not in their graves. Their bodies or their cremated ashes are in their graves, but they—the spirit, the person you know—are with the Lord. In that moment of the Rapture, there will be a reunion of body and spirit. There will be a reunion of our spiritual bodies with our physical bodies. It's hard for me to understand that concept, how all of it will work. We know that to "be absent from the body is to be present with the Lord" (2 Corinthians 5:8). So when we are at the funeral for someone who is a Christian, we can take comfort in knowing that person is with the Lord. But our bodies stay behind and will be resurrected on that day.

These events are so very different from the Second Coming of Jesus. You can't read about the Second Coming of Jesus and think that what we read in 1 Thessalonians 4 has anything to do with the Second Coming. Revelation chapter 19 has some interesting details about what will specifically take place at the Second Coming of Jesus. You won't see anything like a rapture happening. Actually, it's the other way around.

At the Second Coming, we who are Church Age believers will return with Jesus, the King, to the earth.

> I saw heaven standing open and there before me was a white horse, whose rider is called Faithful and True. With justice he judges and wages war. His eyes are like blazing fire, and on his head are many crowns. He has a name written on him that no one knows but he himself. He is dressed in a robe dipped in blood, and his name is the Word of God. The armies of heaven were following him, riding on white horses and dressed in fine linen, white and clean. Coming out of his mouth is a sharp sword with which to strike down the nations. "He will rule them with an iron scepter." He treads the winepress of the fury of the wrath of God Almighty. (Revelation 19:11–15)

He's coming with an army of saints; that's you and me. We'll be dressed in fine, white, clean linen. And we'll be riding white horses. I know this may sound really strange to you, but we're going to be His army coming with Him. I don't think we're going to be doing much in terms of fighting. I have a feeling we might just be cheerleaders for the Lord at that moment. The passage describes a sword that comes from His mouth. That's a way of saying that when Jesus speaks, that's all it will take, and *boom,* all His enemies will be defeated with simply a word. Toward the end of the chapter, it gets really gory. None of this is anything close to what the Rapture will be like. The Rapture is quiet— except for believers—and it's stealthy. There's a mystery involved (more on that in a moment), but not at the Second Coming. Everyone on the planet will see and hear the Second Coming of Christ. It is a completely different event, a completely distinct event.

And then Paul says in 1 Thessalonians 4:18, "Therefore encourage one another with these words." These words that Paul taught about the Rapture were meant to encourage us believers so that when we are going through persecution, we can be comforted to know that this life is not the end. This life is not all there is. Even if my life is difficult and filled with pain or persecution, I have so much to look forward to. It will make everything that goes on in this life pale in comparison, no matter how terrible it is.

As we have said, the Rapture will take place just before what's known as the Tribulation, also identified as the seven-year period the Old Testament prophet Daniel reveals. The book of Revelation talks about the Tribulation, as does Matthew 24. It's also known as the "Day of the Lord" or "that Day" in both the Old and New Testaments. For example, in Hebrews 10:24–25, the author speaks of "the Day" approaching.

> And let us consider how we may spur one another on toward love and good deeds, not giving up meeting together, as some are in the habit of doing, but encouraging one another—and all the more as you see *the Day* approaching. (Hebrews 10:24–25; italics added)

In the book of Revelation, as well as the Old Testament, the "Day of the Lord" suggests a still future fulfillment for the purpose of God pouring out His wrath on unbelievers, specifically aimed at unbelieving Israel, but all other unbelievers will also bear the brunt of this wrath. Look at these references to the "Day of the Lord":

> They are demonic spirits that perform signs, and they go out to the kings of the whole world, to gather them for the battle on *the great day* of God Almighty. (Revelation 16:14; italics added)

> Blow the trumpet in Zion; sound the alarm on my holy hill. Let all who live in the land tremble, for *the day of the Lord* is coming. It is close at hand—*a day* of darkness and gloom, *a day* of clouds and blackness. (Joel 2:1–2a; italics added)

I know all of this might be an overwhelming amount of information. Hopefully, as you compare the differences in the charts (the one here and the one in chapter 2), you'll begin to recognize that one section of

Scripture might deal with one aspect of End Times events, and another passage of Scripture deals with a different aspect of End Times events. Generally speaking, any passage in the Old Testament, and the book of Revelation after chapter 3, will not ever reference the Rapture since it is an event meant only for the Church.

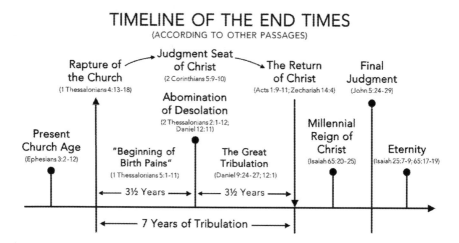

As we talked about in chapter 2, the Rapture is not mentioned, or even hinted at, in Matthew 24–25 in what's known as the Olivet Discourse. Even though you might read through Matthew 24 and think, *Well, that sure looks like the Rapture,* it's not. Everything that's in Matthew 24 refers to something that happens during the Tribulation. It is the context of Matthew 24 that lets us know Jesus is only speaking to the events of the Tribulation in those two chapters.

> And so upon you will come all the righteous blood that has been shed on earth, from the blood of righteous Abel to the blood of Zechariah son of Berekiah, whom you murdered between the temple and the altar. Truly I tell you, all this will come on this generation. Jerusalem, Jerusalem, you who kill the prophets and stone those sent to you, how often I have longed to gather your children together, as a hen gathers her chicks under her wings, and you were not willing. Look, your house is

left to you desolate. For I tell you, you will not see me again until you say, "Blessed is he who comes in the name of the Lord." (Matthew 23:35–39)

In this passage, Jesus is speaking directly to Jewish people about things related to the nation of Israel. The phrase, "all this will come on this generation," was a reference to Jews living during the Tribulation. Remember, the Church is not in view during the Tribulation for it will have been raptured and taken to Heaven before the Tribulation begins.

Now, look at Matthew 24:3: "As Jesus was sitting on the Mount of Olives, the disciples came to him privately. 'Tell us,' they said, 'when will this happen, and what will be the sign of your coming and of the end of the age?'" These are Jewish men asking Jesus when these events that would occur at the end of the age would come to pass. Jesus then answers their question in the rest of chapter 24 and chapter 25. They weren't asking about the Church because they had no clue what the Church was or would come to be. They were asking when God would fulfill His promises to Israel. And that's the question Jesus answered.

As you read Matthew 24–25, particularly verses 38–41 of chapter 24, you have to keep all this in mind. It may look like the Rapture, it may sound like the Rapture, but it's *not* the Rapture. The Rapture is not in evidence there because the Church is not the subject in Matthew 24–25. Verse 37 reminds us that what Jesus has in mind is judgment for the wicked who will be, "swept away," or, "taken away," for judgment, "as it was in the days of Noah," when the people who were swept away were judged for their unbelief. Just as it happened to them, when Jesus returns at the end of the Tribulation, the unbelieving masses will be swept away for judgment. Those who are left will enter the Millennial Kingdom.

CHAPTER 5

OTHER PERSPECTIVES
OF THE RAPTURE

THE BOOK OF REVELATION DOES hint at what's known as the Rapture, but that's all it does. The first three chapters of Revelation contain messages that are intended for the Church. Chapters 2 and 3 of Revelation in particular contain seven messages delivered to seven real churches located in what was then known as Asia Minor. Today that area is part of southwest Turkey. These were churches located in the cities of Ephesus, Smyrna, Pergamum, Thyatira, Sardis, Philadelphia, and Laodicea. But after chapter 3 in the book of Revelation, the Church is never mentioned again. It's as if the Church disappears. Actually, in Revelation chapter 4, after the messages to the seven churches are complete, John writes this: "After this I looked, and there before me was a door standing open in heaven. And the voice I had first heard speaking to me like a trumpet said, 'Come up here, and I will show you what must take place after this'" (Revelation 4:1).

After this moment, the Church seems to disappear. And there is something else that disappears. When Jesus came the first time, He taught us to refer to God as Father. This is an idea that is not prevalent in the Old Testament. Old Testament saints did not think of God as their Father. Jesus introduced the idea in a big way, that in our relationship with God, we can relate to Him as our perfect, heavenly Father. After Revelation chapter 3, the idea of God as Father disappears. That is because in Revelation chapters 4–18, God will be bringing to completion all that He had warned and promised the nation of Israel.

Another passage that speaks about the Rapture is 1 Corinthians 15. It is known as the "resurrection chapter." When you go to church at Easter time, when we celebrate the resurrection of Jesus from the dead, you very well may hear a message containing something out of 1 Corinthians 15. But toward the end of the chapter, Paul talks about something he calls a "mystery." In this context, the word "mystery" is not talking about something shrouded in intrigue. It's not like trying to solve a murder mystery or that kind of thing. The word "mystery" here is a reference to something that was hidden in the past and has now been revealed. The thing that was hidden in the past is the Church. You and I, those of us who are part of the New Testament Church, are not referenced, not even hinted about in the Old Testament. You can study and scour the Old Testament all you want, but the Church is just not there.

When you read through the Old Testament, you might get confused when you read about the prophecy concerning the events surrounding the First Coming of Jesus. That's the Christmas story of the birth of Jesus, coming as a baby in the manger. But Second Coming events are about Jesus coming as King and Lord and Conqueror. The Old Testament prophets saw those two separate events, the First Coming and the Second Coming, as combined into one event. So when you read through the Old Testament, you've got to kind of pick through what you're reading and figure out, "Is it talking about First Coming events, or is it talking about Second Coming events?" It gets confusing at times. Some prophecies in the Old Testament can seem to go back and forth talking about the First Coming and the Second Coming.

Part of what makes it confusing is that the Old Testament prophets didn't see the coming of the Church. That's the mystery. When you read through your New Testament, particularly Paul's letters, you'll see references to this mystery. Here is an example of this language being used:

> Surely you have heard about the administration of God's
> grace that was given to me for you, that is, the *mystery*

made known to me by revelation, as I have already written briefly. In reading this, then, you will be able to understand my insight into the *mystery* of Christ, *which was not made known to people in other generations as it has now been revealed by the Spirit to God's holy apostles and prophets.* This *mystery* is that through the gospel the Gentiles are heirs together with Israel, members together of one body, and sharers together in the promise in Christ Jesus. (Ephesians 3:2–6; italics added)

Note how Paul tells us what the mystery was: Through the gospel, both Jew and Gentile are together in one body, the body of Christ, which is the Church. The Church is not a building. The Church is the people of God gathered.

Notice again what Paul says when talking about the Church, that it, "was not made known to people in other generations as it has now been revealed by the Spirit to God's holy apostles and prophets." The Church was something that was unnoticeable, unseeable in the Old Testament. When Paul references this mystery in 1 Corinthians 15, what he was talking about was the end of the Church Age, something which the Old Testament couldn't foresee.

Listen, I tell you a mystery: We will not all sleep, but we will all be changed—in a flash, in the twinkling of an eye, at the last trumpet. For the trumpet will sound, the dead will be raised imperishable, and we will be changed. For the perishable must clothe itself with the imperishable, and the mortal with immortality. (1 Corinthians 15:51–53)

This is a description of what happens at the end of the Church Age, which is what the Rapture brings. For those of us who are Church Age believers in Christ, it brings to an end our function, our purpose on the planet.

Another big question that comes out of this is, "How is the Rapture going to happen?" What will it look like for someone who has been dead and buried for hundreds of years or longer? Or, let's make it more confusing. What will it look like for someone who was burned to death (think of what happened on September 11, 2001)? What will happen to them? What happens to their bodies? Do they miss out on the resurrection? What about people who were buried at sea, people who eventually became fish food? (I apologize for being crude, but people want to know.) How does that work? How about people who were cremated and their ashes dispersed into the wind? Does any of that frustrate God at all? In terms of God's capability for resurrection, none of that will thwart God's plan for our resurrection.

God, who with His words spoke creation into existence out of nothing, is not frustrated by someone who died at sea or someone burned in a fire or ashes dispersed, or any of those kinds of things. Again, I don't know how to explain it, but there is much about what God has done or will do that I cannot explain. I can't explain how God speaks, and nothing turns into something. I don't understand that at all. I don't understand God without a beginning. But while I may not understand it or be able to explain it, I believe it. We know these things will happen because God's Word makes it very clear. And the promise of God is very clear.

We presented the Rapture as taking place before the Tribulation. But there is a question among Christians as to if that is correct. Some would say it will come *after* the Tribulation. Others would say it will happen at the *midpoint* of the Tribulation. Still others would say that it will happen at some time before God pours out His wrath on the planet. Who is right? To understand the timing of the Rapture, we must understand God's purpose for the Tribulation, that seven-year period before the Second Coming of Christ. This is what the Holy Spirit directed John to write to the church at Philadelphia (this is the ancient Philadelphia located in Asia Minor, not the current-day one in Pennsylvania): "Since you have kept my command to endure patiently, *I will also keep you from the hour of trial that is going to come on the whole world to test the inhabitants of the earth* (Revelation 3:10; italics added). This isn't some small or localized tribulation. No, He is referring to a worldwide event, not something that was going to happen to just that local church in Philadelphia.

Jesus spoke of this event in Matthew 24:21 (the NIV translation uses the word "distress," while others use the word "tribulation"): "For then there will be great distress, unequaled from the beginning of the world until now—and never to be equaled again" (Matthew 24:21). In other words, this will be a worldwide, devastating, all-encompassing event! If you thought 2020 was bad, hang on! That year, or any other time in world history, will seem like a church picnic in comparison. It will be the worst thing this planet has ever seen. Thankfully, we won't have to face this tribulation as, "Since we have now been justified by his blood, how much more shall we be saved from God's wrath through him!" (Romans 5:9).

There are a number of these passages that refer to how God is going to save them from His wrath. Some people would say, "Well, maybe that's talking about Heaven versus hell." But our eternal salvation is not what's in view in these passages.

Let's look at another: "For God did not appoint us to suffer wrath but to receive *salvation* through our Lord Jesus Christ" (1 Thessalonians 5:9; italics added). The context of this passage is the Second Coming. But every time we see the word "salvation" in the New Testament, we automatically think it's a reference to being saved from hell and being able to go to Heaven. But the Greek word for "salvation" is just a regular word. We use it often in our language. We use it to describe what a lifeguard does for someone who's drowning. We use it to describe what a fireman does when someone is inside a burning house. They'll go into the water or the house, and they *rescue* or *save* them. That's what this word means. And in the context of the Second Coming and the wrath of God being poured out on the earth, we Church Age Christians will be *rescued* or *saved* from that wrath because, "God did not appoint us to suffer wrath."

There are Christians today around the world who are being persecuted and martyred for their faith. In a sense, they are experiencing tribulation. Some people put forward an argument that says, "Certainly all these people around the world are experiencing some form of the wrath of God, so who are we to think that we, or the Church in general, will escape that wrath?" And the answer to that question is, "No, they're not experiencing the tribulation or wrath that comes from God." It's not coming from God. If you or I are ever persecuted, if we find ourselves in a nation that hates God and are persecuted for our faith, the context is different. There's a difference between the judgment of humans and the wrath of God.

In this current age, God has appointed governing authorities over us. In some countries, Christians are being jailed and beaten and put to death for their faith in Christ. But that is not the wrath of God. That wrath, or judgment, is coming from a human government that is opposed to God. Humanity's wrath is not the wrath of God. But during the Tribulation, there will be wrath poured out upon the earth that *will* be from God. But Church Age Christians will escape God's wrath. We will be raptured before the beginning of the Tribulation. The answer is found in understanding the purpose of God's wrath. What is God's purpose for bringing wrath during the Tribulation? God's purpose for His wrath will be to demonstrate His judgment on the world for having rejected His Son, Jesus Christ, as Lord and Savior. While the whole world will experience this wrath, it will be particularly focused on the nation of Israel.

Many people will come to trust Christ as Savior during the Tribulation. The book of Revelation references 144,000 specifically called preachers of the message of God. The good news of God will go out to the four corners of the planet, and many will come to a true faith in Christ. But there will also be many who will believe in nominal or superficial ways. This will be another point of the Tribulation. Those who hold to a nominal, superficial, cultural Christianity will have to choose. The Tribulation will force people to decide. There will be no more fence-sitting. People will be given a choice, and it will be very clear. Nobody will be tricked into going to hell. It will be a clear choice. Will you follow and worship the One true God, the Lord Jesus Christ, or will you follow Satan and the Antichrist and take his mark?

The Rapture will bring the Church Age to a close. And God will, once again, deal with Israel during the Tribulation. God has made specific promises to Israel that have yet to be fulfilled. Here is just one of them from 2 Samuel, where the prophet Nathan is speaking for the Lord to King David:

> The Lord declares to you that the Lord himself will
> establish a house for you: When your days are over

and you rest with your ancestors, I will raise up your offspring to succeed you, your own flesh and blood, and I will establish his kingdom. He is the one who will build a house for my Name, and I will establish the throne of his kingdom forever. I will be his father, and he will be my son. When he does wrong, I will punish him with a rod wielded by men, with floggings inflicted by human hands. But my love will never be taken away from him, as I took it away from Saul, whom I removed from before you. Your house and your kingdom will endure forever before me; your throne will be established forever. (2 Samuel 7:11–16)

This prophecy, known as the Davidic covenant, has not yet been fulfilled. God promised David, "Your house and your kingdom will endure forever." That has not yet happened. Did God just decide to not fulfill that promise? Did God just say, "Nah, I'm going to give up on that promise"? That would betray the character of God! Of course, God is going to fulfill His promise to King David and Israel. And during the Tribulation, God will, once again, return to Israel and deal specifically with them. God will deal with their rejection of Jesus as their Messiah, which is the reason for His wrath. The Tribulation will also serve as a precursor to God establishing and fulfilling all these promises that He had made to the nation of Israel.

By the way, the one verse that can sometimes trip us up is 2 Samuel 7:14: "*When he does wrong*, I will punish him with a rod wielded by men, with floggings inflicted by human hands" (italics added). With this being a prophecy fulfilled by Jesus during His first coming, the question arises, how could Jesus be the one "doing wrong?" The misunderstanding has to do with the translation. It's actually not a reference to Jesus somehow *sinning*. It is a reference to the sins of the world *being placed on* Jesus, and Jesus being tortured and killed as a result. When Jesus died for us, He was treated as if He had committed all that sin: "God made him who had no sin to be sin for us so that in him we might become the righteousness of God" (2 Corinthians 5:21).

CHAPTER 6

THE GOSPEL OF THE KINGDOM

ONE OF THE WAYS WE can tell what is happening in Scripture is found in the language of what we are reading. Today we are preaching this thing called the Good News of Jesus Christ. Good news can refer to several things. Good news can be anything good that is happening. When Jesus came and began His public ministry, He proclaimed a specific message. Matthew 4:23 says, "Jesus went throughout Galilee teaching in their synagogues, proclaiming the good news of the kingdom." What was that message? What is the "good news of the kingdom"? The specific message that Jesus was proclaiming is found earlier, in verse 17: "From that time on Jesus began to preach, 'Repent, for the kingdom of heaven has come near'" (Matthew 4:17).

That's the message that Jesus was preaching: "The kingdom of heaven has come near." The Kingdom of God was right in front of them. Jesus represented the Kingdom of God. And if the people of Israel had accepted Him as their Messiah, their King at that point, it would have meant the establishment of the Kingdom.

When you read through the Gospel of Luke, the author kind of hammered that point starting in Luke 9:51: "As the time approached for him to be taken up to heaven, Jesus resolutely set out for Jerusalem." "Jesus set his face toward Jerusalem" (KJV), and everything that is said from that point on in the Gospel of Luke has to be interpreted from the mindset of "The Kingdom of God is at hand. The Kingdom of Heaven is near." It's why you would turn away from your mother and father to follow Jesus. It's why you wouldn't go back and bury your dead loved one. It's why you wouldn't go back for a marriage ceremony. It's why you would stay close to Jesus because, "that moment," was at hand. It's why the messages about Mother and Father, about dead loved ones, and about marriage celebrations don't affect us in the same way. Jesus is not here among us today in the same way. The message we are proclaiming today is not the same. We are not preaching, "Repent. The Kingdom of Heaven is near."

The message we are preaching today is found in Acts 20:24, spoken by the apostle Paul: "My only aim is to finish the race and complete the task the Lord Jesus has given me—the task of testifying to the good news of God's grace." We're not proclaiming the Good News of the Kingdom." We're not saying, "The Kingdom of God is at hand." We're proclaiming the Good News of God's Grace. That message is, "God has sent His Son, Jesus, to come and die for us. He shed His blood for us. He died and rose again for us. And if you would just trust Him as your Lord and Savior, you, too, will be saved, brought into the family of God, and given eternal life." That's the message we're proclaiming right now.

But during the Tribulation, guess what message Christians will be returning to. They're going to return to preaching the Good News of the Kingdom. We see it again in Matthew 24:14, where Jesus is teaching about Tribulation events: "And this gospel of the kingdom will be preached in the whole world as a testimony to all nations, and then the end will come."

The message they will be preaching during the Tribulation is the same message Jesus preached during His earthly ministry: "The Kingdom of God is at hand. The Kingdom of Heaven is near." The fulfillment of this verse will not happen until the end of the Tribulation. And they will know how near the Kingdom will be because the Tribulation will last about seven years. They will be able to figure out when it started, and they will know approximately how long they have until Jesus comes. All they will have to do is read it right in the Bible and know the timing of it all. Now, they won't know the day or the hour, but they will know that it will be about seven years from when it started. They will be able to know the start of the Tribulation by when, "all those Christians disappeared," (the Rapture).

Second Thessalonians tells us that many people will be deceived during the time of the Tribulation: "For this reason *God sends them a powerful delusion* so that they will believe the lie and so that all will be condemned who have not believed the truth but have delighted in wickedness" (2 Thessalonians 2:11–12; (italics added). This is the reason people won't be running to their Bibles to figure out what happened. The prevalent thought will be, *We need a world leader who can fix this for us.* And they won't know what to do. Then the Antichrist will step into that void. It will be peaceful for a while; it might be wonderful during that time. And then halfway through the Tribulation, the Antichrist will climb the steps up to the Temple in Jerusalem and say, "I am God. You must worship me."

> Don't let anyone deceive you in any way, for that day will not come until the rebellion occurs and the man of lawlessness is revealed, the man doomed to destruction. *He will oppose and will exalt himself over everything that is called God or is worshiped, so that he sets himself up in God's temple, proclaiming himself to be God.* (2 Thessalonians 2:3–4; italics added)

It will be at that time when Israel, almost in unison, will recognize that they missed it. It will be as if the blinders fell from their eyes. So many people will come to faith in Christ in that moment. And many of those will lose their heads, literally, because of the wrath of Satan expressed through the Antichrist. It will be the Gospel of the Kingdom that will be declared during this very terrible time. The Tribulation will be most severe, but the good news will be that it's all about to end. Hang on! The Kingdom is near; it is at hand! Jesus will be here very soon!

> After this I looked, and there before me was a great multitude that no one could count, from every nation, tribe, people and language, standing before the throne

and before the Lamb. They were wearing white robes and were holding palm branches in their hands. And they cried out in a loud voice: "Salvation belongs to our God, who sits on the throne, and to the Lamb."…Then one of the elders asked me, "These in white robes who are they, and where did they come from?" I answered, "Sir, you know." And he said, "These are they who have come out of the great tribulation; they have washed their robes and made them white in the blood of the Lamb. (Revelation 7:9–10, 13–14)

Now, one more question concerning the Rapture: What will happen to the Church Age saints after the Rapture? It will certainly be different from what will be happening on the planet during the Tribulation. But for us, there will be two main events that we, as Church Age saints, will be looking forward to. One is called the Judgment Seat of Christ. This judgment is only intended for Church Age believers because the only people who will be involved in the Rapture are the Church. It won't be for Old Testament saints as they will not be raised at the Rapture. The Bible specifically teaches that they will be resurrected at the Second Coming of Jesus. So it will be New Testament saints. That's it.

Paul refers to the Judgment Seat of Christ in a few places:

For we will all stand before God's judgment seat. It is written: "As surely as I live," says the Lord, "every knee will bow before me; every tongue will acknowledge God." So then, each of us will give an account of ourselves to God. (Romans 14:10c–12)

For we must all appear before the judgment seat of Christ, so that each of us may receive what is due us for the things done while in the body, whether good or bad. (2 Corinthians 5:10)

This is not a judgment for sin. When you stand before the Lord on this day, you will not be answering for your sin. Your sin was already answered for at the cross by Jesus. Your sin has already been judged. It has already been paid for. It was paid for by Jesus when He died on the cross for you!

The Judgment Seat of Christ will be a judgment for something else:

> If anyone builds on this foundation using gold, silver, costly stones, wood, hay or straw, their work will be shown for what it is, because the Day will bring it to light. It will be revealed with fire, and the fire will test the quality of each person's work. If what has been built survives, the builder will *receive a reward*. If it is burned up, the builder *will suffer loss but yet will be saved*—even though only as one escaping through the flames. (1 Corinthians 3:12–15; italics added)

This judgment is reserved for believers. It will be a judgment for the works you accomplished here on the earth. How did you live your life? Did you serve others? Did you serve in the local church? Did you serve with a loving, unselfish attitude? Were you generous in your support of your local church? Were your motives pure, or did you serve or give to receive recognition or for other selfish reasons? These will be the things we will be giving an account for during the Judgment Seat of Christ.

The second event that will happen after the Rapture is called the Marriage Supper of the Lamb, or the Wedding Supper of the Lamb. What a celebration that will be! The reference to this is found in Revelation 19:6–9:

> Then I heard what sounded like a great multitude, like the roar of rushing waters and like loud peals of thunder, shouting: "Hallelujah! For our Lord God Almighty reigns. Let us rejoice and be glad and give him glory! For the wedding of the Lamb has come, and his bride has made herself ready. Fine linen, bright and clean, was given her to wear." (Fine linen stands for the righteous acts of God's holy people.) Then the angel said to me,

"Write this: Blessed are those who are invited to the wedding supper of the Lamb!" And he added, "These are the true words of God."

The bride spoken of in this passage is the Church. That's us! We are the Bride of Christ. His bride has made herself ready and will be dressed in fine white linen. This is why when we have weddings, the bride dresses in white. In Ephesians 5, in Paul's instruction to husbands, he says this:

Husbands, love your wives, just as Christ loved the church and gave himself up for her to make her holy, cleansing her by the washing with water through the word, and to present her to himself as a radiant church, without stain or wrinkle or any other blemish, but holy and blameless. (Ephesians 5:25–27)

These things may all sound far-fetched to you. You may be tempted to think, *It's been so long, I don't think Jesus is coming back.* Let me assure you these events will most certainly take place!

Above all, you must understand that in the last days scoffers will come, scoffing and following their own evil desires. They will say, "Where is this 'coming' He promised? Ever since our ancestors died, everything goes on as it has since the beginning of creation." … The Lord is not slow in keeping his promise, as some understand slowness. Instead he is patient with you, not wanting anyone to perish, but everyone to come to repentance. But the day of the Lord will come like a thief. (2 Peter 3:3–4, 9–10a)

Here we're told to be patient because the Lord is not slow in keeping His promise. Why is God waiting? It's not so much that God is being slow. Rather, He is being patient, not willing for anyone to perish, to die without Christ, but that all will come to repentance and faith in Jesus Christ. And when that happens and the time is right for the Rapture to take place, that's when it will happen. It may not be when we want it to happen. I would just encourage you to be ready because it is imminent. Are there any relationships that you would like to see restored before that day comes? Are there any situations that need to be dealt with before that day arrives? It could happen at any moment, and you don't want to be caught unprepared for that day!

SECTION 3

THE OLIVET DISCOURSE

CHAPTER 7

SETTING THE SCENE

In this section, we deal specifically with Matthew chapters 24 and 25, which cover the events of the Tribulation. In terms of the order of End Times events, the Tribulation is the sandwich meat between the bread of the Rapture and the Second Coming of Christ. Matthew 24 doesn't address the Rapture, as we discovered earlier, but it does end with the coming of Jesus as King to the planet.

Before we dive into Matthew 24 and look at what's called the Olivet Discourse, we need to go back to Matthew 23 to understand some context issues. As we covered in chapter 3 of this book, trying to understand Scripture without its context will generally lead to a whole world of trouble. In this section, we reveal a portion of Scripture and then discuss it. We follow that pattern through chapter 24.

About halfway through chapter 23, Jesus began to address the teachers of the law and the Pharisees. These were the guys assigned the task of identifying the promised Messiah for everyone else in all Israel. The people were looking to their religious leaders to help them. Their task not only involved identifying the Messiah, they were also responsible for vetting Him. The people trusted the teachers of the law and the Pharisees to recognize who the Messiah might be. They certainly didn't want to miss His appearance! But they all failed miserably.

It wasn't so much that they didn't recognize that Jesus was the Messiah. I believe most of them did recognize that Jesus was from God, but they wanted to reserve power and authority for themselves.

Because of their egos and selfishness, the teachers of the law and the Pharisees didn't want to recognize Jesus as the Messiah. So they plotted to kill Him.

Now, don't forget the sovereignty of God: Their rejection of Jesus was laid out before the foundation of the world. God knew what would happen to humankind. He knew that sin would be introduced into the world. He knew that we would need a Messiah, a Savior. All this was set forth before the foundation of the world. In Matthew 23, Jesus addresses these religious leaders with seven "woes," seven announcements of coming doom. Jesus uses some abrupt language with them. It's quite harsh. See if you agree with me as you look at the first two woes:

> Woe to you, teachers of the law and Pharisees, you hypocrites! You shut the door of the kingdom of heaven in people's faces. You yourselves do not enter, nor will you let those enter who are trying to. Woe to you, teachers of the law and Pharisees, you hypocrites! You travel over land and sea to win a single convert, and when you have succeeded, you make them twice as much a child of hell as you are. (Matthew 23:13–15)

Jesus doesn't beat around the bush when He addresses these religious leaders. His language was certainly not nice or kind. It's really in your face. Let's continue:

> You snakes! You brood of vipers! How will you escape being condemned to hell? Therefore I am sending you prophets and sages and teachers. Some of them you will kill and crucify; others you will flog in your synagogues and pursue from town to town. And so upon you will come all the righteous blood that has been shed on earth, from the blood of righteous Abel to the blood of Zechariah son of Berekiah, whom you murdered between the temple and the altar. Truly I tell you, all this will come on this generation. (Matthew 23:33–36)

Jesus calls them hypocrites, snakes, a brood of vipers. He tells them that they won't escape being condemned to hell. Wow! That's about as in your face as you can get. And then here, Jesus takes on the role of a prophet. He prophesies something that would happen in their current context. Jesus spoke of sending them "prophets and sages." These are New Testament prophets and sages He is talking about. "Some of them you will kill and crucify"; this can't be a reference to Old Testament prophets because they didn't crucify any Old Testament prophets, but they would crucify New Testament ones. "Others you will flog in your synagogues"; there weren't any synagogues in the Old Testament, so again, this was a reference to synagogues in their day.

The apostle Paul, in his former life as Saul the Pharisee, participated in some of this persecution before he met Jesus on the road to Damascus. And then Jesus said, "upon you will come all the righteous blood that has been shed on the earth." In other words, you will be held accountable. Partly because all of these Old Testament prophets who came before in Israel, you put them to death. And now these New Testament prophets, you will be putting them to death. All this will come upon you, "from the blood of righteous Abel to the blood of Zechariah, son of Berekiah, whom you murdered between the temple and the altar." Jesus is referring to all these Old Testament prophets starting with Abel, who was killed by Cain, and then finally, Zechariah, the last of the Old Testament prophets who were murdered. "Truly, I tell you all this will come on this generation." All of this judgment and woe will come upon that generation. It won't be us, the Church Age believers.

The next part of the passage might sound like a familiar refrain:

> Jerusalem, Jerusalem, you who kill the prophets and stone those sent to you, how often I have longed to gather your children together, as a hen gathers her chicks under her wings, and you were not willing. Look, your house is left to you desolate. For I tell you, you will not see me again until you say, "Blessed is he who comes in the name of the Lord." (Matthew 23:37–39)

God sent messengers and prophets to Jerusalem and Israel over and over again. And His chosen nation kept rejecting them. They kept murdering them. Notice the last phrase, "Blessed is he who comes in the name of the Lord." This is what they were shouting at Jesus on what we know as Palm Sunday when He was riding a donkey into the city of Jerusalem. This is what they will be shouting when Jesus comes to set up the Kingdom. Jesus said you won't hear that again until the day of the Second Coming of Christ.

As you come into chapter 24, understand that Jesus is not through with the nation of Israel. At an unknown future time, Jesus will return. At that point, Israel will accept Him, not reject Him as they did at His first coming. It may be hard to believe, but there will be a time when Israel will accept Jesus Christ as their Messiah. Now, let's look at the beginning of Matthew 24:

> Jesus left the temple and was walking away when his disciples came up to him to call his attention to its buildings. "Do you see all these things?" he asked. "Truly I tell you, not one stone here will be left on another; every one will be thrown down." (Matthew 24:1–2)

What Jesus announced to His disciples here would have been shocking to their ears. The Temple in Jerusalem represented their security. That was true for almost every Israelite. Their security didn't come from their relationship with God at all, but from the Temple in Jerusalem itself. Its fortifications and walls around the city represented their security. A secondary application for us is that we should not find our security in Washington DC. Our security is not in those buildings or the halls of Congress or the White House. Our security is found in our heavenly Father, the relationship He has provided to us through His Son, Jesus Christ!

The next verse is also key to understanding these two chapters: "As Jesus was sitting on the Mount of Olives, the disciples came to him privately. 'Tell us,' they said, 'when will this happen, and what will be the sign of your coming and of the end of the age?'" (Matthew 24:3).

At this point they were situated on the Mount of Olives, which is on a hill outside Jerusalem that overlooks the city with its gates, the Temple, and surrounding buildings. They would have been able to see the pinnacle of the Temple, and the sight of it all would have been beautiful. This would have been a peaceful and inspiring setting. And Jesus had just told them it was all going to be destroyed!

As Jesus was sitting in that beautiful place, the disciples came to Him and asked two questions. The first question was, "Tell us when this will happen?" They were confused and alarmed. They had just heard Jesus condemn the teachers of the law and the Pharisees. They heard Jesus pronounce all the "woes" on them and that they were going to hell. That all of this would come on this generation. When was all this going to happen? The second question was, "What will be the sign of Your coming and the end of the age?" In other words, "How will we know when it's time for You to come again?" And this is the context for the rest of chapters 24 and 25.

TIMELINE OF THE END TIMES
(ACCORDING TO MATTHEW 24–25)

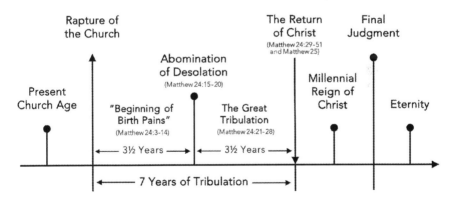

CHAPTER 8

EVENTS DURING THE TRIBULATION

SOME PEOPLE MAY REFER TO the Olivet Discourse as a sermon, but it's not. For Jesus, there was no preparation in the way that a pastor prepares to preach a sermon. These two chapters are extemporaneous. Jesus could pull this off because He's Jesus. What is known as the Olivet Discourse is just Jesus answering in response to their two questions: "When will this happen?" and "What will be the sign of Your coming at the end of the age?" That's what we want to know. We must also remember that Jesus is speaking specifically to Israel. He's speaking *about* Israel, and He's speaking *to* Israel. The whole context of this passage, beginning in chapter 23, is Jesus speaking to Israel.

What you won't find in chapter 24 is any reference to the Church. We are living in the Church Age today. So when the disciples asked the questions about the coming of the end of the age, it's not our age that's in view. It's not the Church Age they're asking about. They don't even understand the concept of the Church yet. They had no clue. That so-called mystery had not yet been revealed to them. Jesus had kind of lobbed a little bit of an information grenade at them back in Matthew 16:18, when He told them, "And I tell you that you are Peter, and on this rock I will build my church, and the gates of Hades will not overcome it." The disciples didn't have a clue what Jesus was talking about. We can understand it better because we get to look back over the events after they happened, but they were living these events. The idea of the

Rapture is not in view here at all either because it is an event specifically for Church Age believers.

Let's buckle up now because we are going to go through this next portion, and it's going to be a pretty rough ride. This is what's known as the Tribulation. Thank the Lord, you and I will not have to see it other than whatever view we may have from Heaven. At the beginning of the Tribulation, there will be an uneasy peace. (Jesus doesn't reference it here in Matthew 24, but we'll see it in Revelation.) But the situation will deteriorate quickly. There are three parts of the Tribulation: the first half, the middle point, and then the second half of the Tribulation, which culminates with the Second Coming of Christ. So in verse 4, Jesus begins to answer their questions:

> Jesus answered: "Watch out that no one deceives you. For many will come in my name, claiming, 'I am the Messiah,' and will deceive many. You will hear of wars and rumors of wars, but see to it that you are not alarmed. Such things must happen, but the end is still to come. Nation will rise against nation, and kingdom against kingdom. There will be famines and earthquakes in various places. All these are the beginning of birth pains." (Matthew 24:4–8)

Jesus begins by giving a warning. He gives this warning three times: at the beginning, at the midpoint, and the end. This warning corresponds to all three parts of the Tribulation. And here is another secondary application for us. We need to be vigilant in recognizing and calling out false prophets or false messiahs because they're everywhere. We must be aware of that—even in our age, the Church Age. Remember that the wars and rumors of wars, famines, and earthquakes are not things to be looking for in our age. We may see wars and famines and earthquakes, but there will be something about their intensity or size or location that will be unique during the Tribulation.

Then Jesus said, "All these are the beginning of birth pains." Thankfully, I haven't experienced birth pains. Apparently, it's not fun stuff. I am happy to remain in my ignorance about the subject. Now let me ask a question. When a woman is carrying a child, does she have any idea when that child will be born? I'm speaking in general terms, in terms of weeks or maybe months. As a pregnant mother is getting along in months, getting toward the end, she has at least a general idea of when the baby will come. It's going to be somewhere around the due date the doctor gave her, right? It sometimes doesn't work out that way, but it's close. There are some clues along the way that something's coming. As they get closer to the delivery, the birth pains start to increase. As the pains increase in frequency and intensity, she knows it's coming. And at some point, the baby is like, "Ready or not, here I come!" And it hurts, right?

This is not a description of what happens as we await the Rapture. We talked about how the Rapture is an imminent event. It could happen at any moment. That's not true when it comes to pregnancy. Now you might have an early delivery for your pregnancy, but once you get pregnant, there's a countdown clock. You kind of know about when the baby will come. That's true of the Tribulation. When the Tribulation begins, those who become followers of Jesus during that period will be able to pick up a Bible, read these passages, and figure out, "Okay, we've got seven years." That's how long the Tribulation will last. And the closer and closer and closer you get to the end of the Tribulation, the more and more "birth" pains there will be. That's what Jesus tells us to look for.

And then, at the middle point of the Tribulation, the Antichrist will break the peace agreement with Israel, which he bargained with them at the beginning of the Tribulation. We'll see more about this in Revelation.

> Then you will be handed over to be persecuted and put to death, and you will be hated by all nations because of me. At that time many will turn away from the faith and will betray and hate each other, and many false prophets will appear and deceive many people. Because of the increase of wickedness, the love of most will grow cold, but the one who stands firm to the end will be saved. And this gospel of the kingdom will be preached

in the whole world as a testimony to all nations, and then the end will come. (Matthew 24:9–14)

The Antichrist will bring great persecution on Israel and any who might come to their aid. Israel will be the focal point of the Antichrist's and the rest of the world's rage. This is why today you see a rise in anti-Semitism. Don't ever be surprised by the rise in anti-Semitism. Even though the world experienced many horrific things, like what Hitler did to the Jews during World War II, don't be surprised when anti-Semitism rears its head. Anti-Semitism has been going on all the way back to Abraham in the book of Genesis, and it will be even worse during the Tribulation. Those who become followers of Christ during the Tribulation, even Gentiles, will be associated with the Jews and persecuted along with Israel. Many Christians and Jews will be slaughtered during the Tribulation.

During the Tribulation, many will turn away from *the* faith, the true Christian faith, because it will be too hard to follow. Jesus said, "They will betray and hate each other. Many false prophets will appear and deceive many people." And then He said, "The one who stands firm to the end will be saved." Again, as we discussed earlier, this is not talking about eternal or heavenly salvation. This is talking about saving your life, your physical life. "Those who stand firm to the end," is not a description of what it takes for someone to be saved eternally. Eternal salvation comes through faith in Christ. It is by grace, through faith in Christ that we become saved for eternity. Standing firm to the end is talking about the saving of your physical life through the Tribulation.

Remember, the Gospel of the Kingdom, as we mentioned previously, is not the gospel that we are preaching now. The gospel that we're preaching now is called the Gospel of Grace. The Gospel of the Kingdom is the gospel that Jesus preached during His public ministry here on the earth. Christians living during the Tribulation will once again be preaching this gospel. Why? Because the Kingdom of God will be at hand; it will be near. And Christians living during this time will know about how many months or years they have before the return of Jesus. Sometimes mission organizations or evangelistic associations (Billy Graham's organization, for instance) take Matthew 24:14 out of context and say, "Jesus won't come back until we preach the gospel to the whole world." While it is our—the Church's—responsibility to take the gospel to the world, the prophecy of verse 14 describes a specific event at the end of the Tribulation.

As mentioned previously, during the Tribulation, there will be a special provision for the 144,000 witnesses who will have the stamp of God, the mark of God, on their foreheads. They will go and proclaim the message of this Gospel of the Kingdom. They will be protected from the Antichrist's harm (we'll see them when we look at the book of Revelation). So this Gospel of the Kingdom will be declared throughout the whole world. And then the end will come.

And now comes the full-blown revealing of the Antichrist. This is the actual midpoint of the Tribulation:

> So when you see standing in the holy place "the abomination that causes desolation," spoken of through the prophet Daniel—let the reader understand—then let those who are in Judea flee to the mountains. Let no one on the housetop go down to take anything out of the house. Let no one in the field go back to get their cloak. How dreadful it will be in those days for pregnant women and nursing mothers! Pray that your flight will not take place in winter or on the Sabbath. For then there will be great distress, unequaled from the beginning of the world until now—and never to be equaled again. (Matthew 24:15–21)

This almost sounds like a monster movie, right? It's almost like Godzilla shows up. But no, this is what Scripture calls, "the Abomination of Desolation."

> He will confirm a covenant with many for one "seven." In the middle of the "seven" he will put an end to sacrifice and offering. And at the temple he will set up an abomination that causes desolation, until the end that is decreed is poured out on him. (Daniel 9:27)

This is a reference to the Antichrist. The Antichrist will strike some sort of peace deal or covenant for "one seven," seven years. In the middle of those seven years, at the middle point of the Tribulation, he will put an end to sacrifice in what will be a rebuilt Temple in Jerusalem. He will then set up an "abomination that causes desolation," which is himself climbing the steps of the Temple and declaring himself to be God and that the world must now worship him. At that point, millions of Jews will have the veil lifted, their eyes will be opened, and they will declare, "We missed it! Our Messiah has been Jesus all this time and we missed it!" Now they're in trouble. That's why Jesus tells them next, "Then let those who are in Judea flee to the mountains." The message is, "Run, or you will die!" "Let no one on the housetop go down and take anything out of the house." Why? Because you're running for your life!

"How dreadful it will be in those days for pregnant women and nursing mothers." This is just a statement of fact. If someone happens to be pregnant during the Tribulation, it will not be good for them. "Pray that your flight will not take place in winter or on the Sabbath." Why? Because traveling in the winter can be tough. Especially if it will be hard to buy things like gas or groceries, which it will be. It will also be bad because Jews can only travel a very short distance on the Sabbath because of the Mosaic law. The distress of these days will be unequaled to anything the world has seen or will ever see in all of history. If you thought the Holocaust was bad, or some other time when many atrocities were committed, just wait until this time during the Tribulation.

This is a harsh message from the Scriptures. The best way to understand this is that the world will be the domain of Satan's man during this time.

> If those days had not been cut short, no one would survive, but for the sake of the elect those days will be shortened. At that time if anyone says to you, "Look, here is the Messiah!" or, "There he is!" do not believe it. For false messiahs and false prophets will appear and perform great signs and wonders to deceive, if possible, even the elect. See, I have told you ahead of time. So if

anyone tells you, "There he is, out in the wilderness," do not go out; or, "Here he is, in the inner rooms," do not believe it. (Matthew 24:22–26)

Once again, we see Jesus warn about the rise of false prophets and false messiahs who will gather people to follow them and deceive many. But when Jesus appears, He will come quickly. It will be fast. It will be visible. It will be loud. Everyone on the planet will witness this event. Everyone will know this is the one and only true Messiah. The purpose of this all is judgment. Jesus, the righteous Judge, will make things right. That's a big part of what the Tribulation is all about. He also talks about how the false prophets and false messiahs will be able to perform great signs and wonders. These are not *fake* signs and wonders; these are *great* signs and wonders. Many people will be deceived because of them. For those people who are alive during the Tribulation, be aware! Is it possible someone could pick up this book or another one like it and be able to figure some of these things out? That would be awesome!

CHAPTER 9

THE END OF THE TRIBULATION

Jesus CONTINUES TO DESCRIBE EVENTS associated with the end of the Tribulation:

> For as lightning that comes from the east is visible even in the west, so will be the coming of the Son of Man. Wherever there is a carcass, there the vultures will gather. Immediately after the distress of those days "the sun will be darkened, and the moon will not give its light; the stars will fall from the sky, and the heavenly bodies will be shaken." Then will appear the sign of the Son of Man in heaven. And then all the peoples of the earth will mourn when they see the Son of Man coming on the clouds of heaven, with power and great glory. And he will send his angels with a loud trumpet call, and they will gather his elect from the four winds, from one end of the heavens to the other. (Matthew 24:27–31)

Jesus said, "I've told you ahead of time, be ready, for as lightning that comes from the east is visible even in the west so will be the coming of the Son of Man." Again, these are not words associated with the Rapture. This is talking about the Second Coming of Christ. Every eye will see Him. I don't know how that will work. If Jesus shows up in Jerusalem, which is where He is going to show up, I don't know how people in China will see Him or how people in South America will see Him. I don't understand the mechanics of that event. But it will happen! And it will be loud. And vultures are going to gather there because carcasses will be piled up high there. Immediately after the distress of those days, the sun will be darkened. The moon will not give its light. Stars will fall from the sky, and heavenly bodies will be shaken. Then will appear the sign of the Son of Man in heaven. All the peoples of the earth will mourn when they see Jesus coming on the clouds with power and with great glory. Except for those who are Christians. They will be celebrating. Believers in Christ will be cheering the moment. But those who are not will watch in terror. It will be devastating for them. This will be a universal event.

There will be angels with a loud trumpet call. They will gather His elect from the four winds, from one end of the heavens to the other. Now some will look at this and say, "Now there's your Rapture. It means the Rapture will happen at the very end." All this information may be confusing, but this is not the Rapture. At the end of the Tribulation, there will be many other rapture-like events. One of these events will be when all the peoples of the world are gathered for a time of judgment. The parables of Matthew 25 deal with these events. The primary application of Matthew 24–25 is for a future generation that is not us.

We may be able to glean some secondary applications from Matthew 24–25 for our benefit. But understand, Jesus is speaking these things, the apostle Matthew recorded them, and the Holy Spirit inspired all of this, but mostly for the benefit of those who would be going through the Tribulation. And that's not Church Age believers. We struggle with that because we think everything must be all about us. We're selfish that way. When someone writes something down, we think it must be about us or me. What are they saying about me? What are they saying about us? But Matthew 24–25 is not directed toward us at all. It is directed toward that future generation who will be experiencing the Tribulation.

Back in Matthew 24, Jesus gives another parable to illustrate His Second Coming:

> Now learn this lesson from the fig tree: As soon as its twigs get tender and its leaves come out, you know that

summer is near. Even so, when you see all these things, you know that it is near, right at the door. Truly I tell you, this generation will certainly not pass away until all these things have happened. Heaven and earth will pass away, but my words will never pass away. But about that day or hour no one knows, not even the angels in heaven, nor the Son, but only the Father. (Matthew 24:32–36)

At this point in Matthew 24, the Tribulation is just about over. We've been through just about the whole thing. And Jesus says, "Now learn this lesson from the fig tree: As soon as its twigs get tender and its leaves come out, you know that summer is near." Right? That's kind of how it works. As the winter turns to spring, you can tell what's coming. Summer's coming. As soon as the twigs get tender and the leaves start popping out, you know that summer is on its way. Is that an indefinite period? Or do we kind of know how long it will be before summer arrives? It's not like the Rapture, which is imminent, meaning it could happen at any moment. It could be five days from now, it could be five months from now, it could be five hundred years from now. But summer doesn't just pop up. The arrival of summer doesn't surprise us. We know that it's coming. There are clues. Jesus said when you see the clues illustrated by an expectant mother or by the changing of the seasons, those clues are pointing to the return of Christ at the end of the Tribulation.

"Truly I tell you this generation will certainly not pass away until all these things have happened." The generation Jesus was speaking of was not the generation He was speaking to at that particular moment. It is not our generation either. The generation Jesus was referring to is the future generation, who will be experiencing all these events of the Tribulation. That future generation will not pass away until all the events of the Tribulation that Jesus described come to pass. Because it's only going to take seven years. So it is very reasonable for Jesus to say, "This generation will not pass away." Again, it has nothing to do with us.

"But about that day or hour no one knows, not even the angels in heaven, nor the Son, but only the Father." Again, this phrase is not a reference to the Rapture. It's a reference to the Second Coming of Jesus because He is talking about days and hours. They will know the approximate time of Christ's return. They will have an idea. It will be seven years from the beginning of the Tribulation, which follows the Rapture. They will be able to identify the middle point of the Tribulation, which will happen three and a half years before the Second Coming of Jesus. But they won't know the exact day or hour when it will happen. They will have to be ready.

Jesus goes on to talk about the days of Noah:

> As it was in the days of Noah, so it will be at the coming of the Son of Man. For in the days before the flood, people were eating and drinking, marrying and giving in marriage, up to the day Noah entered the ark; and they knew nothing about what would happen until the flood came and took them all away. That is how it will be at the coming of the Son of Man. Two men will be in the field; one will be taken and the other left. Two women will be grinding with a hand mill; one will be taken and the other left. Therefore keep watch, because you do not know on what day your Lord will come. (Matthew 24:37–42)

What happened in the days of Noah? There was a *big* event in the days of Noah. Do you remember what that was? There was a flood, a universal flood. Noah and his family entered the ark. Noah had been proclaiming, "There's a flood coming!" But the people refused to believe it. They hadn't even seen rain yet. They thought that old man Noah was not in his right mind. "Go ahead, get on your big boat out there in the middle of dry land." They did this until the day the flood came. They knew nothing about what would happen until the flood came. And what did the flood do? It took them all away. It, in a sense, "raptured" them. It swept them away for judgment.

Jesus teaches here that is how it will be at the coming of the Son of Man. The flood swept away—raptured—those who were lost and ungodly. Noah and his family stayed behind on the ark and went into the new world that came after the flood. But the lost were taken away. Where to? We don't see the answer here in Matthew 24, but we do in a parallel passage in Luke 17:

> "I tell you, on that night two people will be in one bed; one will be taken and the other left. Two women will be grinding grain together; one will be taken and the other left." "Where, Lord?" they asked. He replied, *"Where there is a dead body, there the vultures will gather."* (Luke 17:34–37; italics added)

This rapture-like event takes or sweeps away all the unsaved at the end of the Tribulation. The vultures will gather where death and destruction will take place. Read the end of Revelation 19 for a description of what is called the "Great Supper of God." It's very gruesome. For sure, you don't want an invitation to that supper! This is what will happen to all the unsaved, those who are without Christ, at the end of the Tribulation when Jesus comes again.

Jesus ended this discussion with four parables, one at the end of chapter 24 (the parable of the faithful servant and the evil servant) and three in chapter 25. In chapter 25, there's the parable of the ten virgins. There's the parable of the talents (the NIV refers to them as bags of gold). A talent is a measure of something. Finally, there's the parable about the sheep and the goats. I graduated from high school in 1982, just before Christian music artist Keith Green died. You may not remember Keith Green. You may have to be of a certain age. He had a song called "The Sheep and the Goats," which I love. But it does have a wrong application to the parable. The lyrics speak to the idea that we Church Age believers will be at this judgment. But again, this is an event that will happen at the end of the Tribulation. You and I won't be there.

While none of the parables in Matthew 25 pertain to us directly, there are secondary applications for us. All three parables speak to the believer's faithfulness. Each one describes the actions the characters took and then the judgment they received based on those actions. The ten virgins needed to provide oil for their lamps. Those who neglected to get extra oil for their lamps missed out on the coming of the Groom. The parable of the talents was based on how the servants invested what God had given them. And the parable of the sheep and the goats was about the people being judged by how they treated those who were less fortunate. But none of those things are how we come to be saved, which is through faith in Christ. Just as with us, these Tribulation saints are not saved because of their actions or the things they accomplished. That would be contrary to how both Old and New Testament saints were saved. But their actions did reveal a life that was faithful or full of faith. In other words, these Tribulation saints took those faithful actions *because of* their faith.

The parable of the ten virgins is, specifically, a judgment for living Jews at the end of the Tribulation. It talks about whether these people are saved or not. It will have nothing to do with you or me. Those who are saved, as evidenced by their faithfulness, will go into the Millennial Kingdom; those who are not saved will be killed at that point and reserved for future judgment. The parable of the talents was, again, a judgment for living Jews having to do with reward. The size and quality of their rewards in the Millennial Kingdom would be based on their faithfulness in properly carrying out God's will in what God had blessed them with. Finally, the parable of the sheep and the goats deals with the judgment of living Gentiles after the Tribulation. And it will deal with both salvation and reward because it talks about how those who are faithful would be given greater assignments and many rewards in the Millennial Kingdom. And how the goats, who represent lost people, will suffer in eternal punishment.

A lot of information has been given in this section. You might feel like you've been standing on the receiving end of a fire hose of information. But let's end this section with this. We know Jesus is coming again. We know these events will happen. One of the ways we know this is because of His first coming. There were so many prophecies in the Old Testament that foretold of the First Coming of Jesus. Some of those prophecies were told hundreds of years, some a thousand years before Jesus came. Not only do we have a lot of Old Testament prophecies foretelling His Second Coming, here we have Jesus himself as a New Testament prophet talking about how He will come again.

This time Jesus will not be coming as a baby in a manger but as the King who will execute His righteous judgment. And it won't be according to what *we think* is fair or right.

For those of us who are followers of Christ, we say "Amen, may it be so! Come quickly, Lord Jesus!" That's how John ends the book of Revelation. We don't need to wait anymore. We're looking forward to that day when Jesus, our Lord and Savior, comes again. The next event on the prophetic calendar is for us Church Age believers to escape out of here in the Rapture. It is proper for us to look forward to that. The word *Maranatha*, translated as "Come, Lord" in 1 Corinthians 16:22, is the Aramaic way early Christians used to greet each other. You might have heard it before. It voices a belief and a hope that Jesus would soon return. Lord, come quickly! Come get us! We look forward to Your coming!

SECTION 4

FROM THE PERSPECTIVE OF REVELATION

CHAPTER 10

BLOCKBUSTER AT THE
MOVIE THEATER

This is the section where we go through the book of Revelation. We'll be referring to another chart; this is the third. We've already looked at the chart based on the Olivet Discourse (Matthew 24–25). The second chart is based on several assorted passages, including 1 and 2 Thessalonians, and 1 Corinthians. In this chapter, we'll introduce the third chart, this one based on events in the book of Revelation.

TIMELINE OF THE END TIMES
(ACCORDING TO REVELATION)

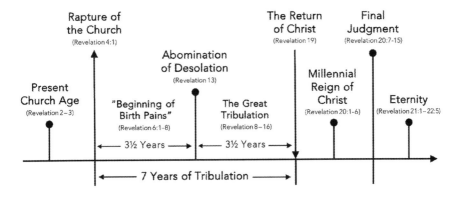

There is a distinction between the Church and Israel. We are living in the Church Age. God was specifically dealing with the nation of Israel during Old Testament times. When the Church was established, there was a transition period. The book of Acts covers the transition between God's dealing with Israel and the introduction of the Church and how it became the main focus of God's attention. God will one day bring the Church Age to its conclusion with the event that we know as the Rapture, which will serve as the kickoff event for what's known as the Tribulation or the Day of the Lord.

> "Whoever has ears, let them hear what the Spirit says to the churches." After this I looked, and there before me was a door standing open in heaven. And the voice I had first heard speaking to me like a trumpet said, "Come up here, and I will show you what must take place after this." At once I was in the Spirit, and there before me was a throne in heaven with someone sitting on it. (Revelation 3:22–4:2)

While the book of Revelation doesn't address the Rapture directly, it does hint at it. And that's what we find in this passage. Jesus had been speaking through the apostle John to the seven churches of Asia Minor (modern-day Turkey). There's something about the timing here because from this point forward, there is no more mention of the Church. It seems to be removed between chapter 3 and chapter 4 of Revelation. Revelation 4:1 uses what sounds like language that would be used to describe the Rapture.

From this point on in the book of Revelation, we won't hear of two things. One, as already mentioned, is the Church. One obvious reason is that the Church, at that point, is gone. The second thing you won't hear about is the concept of God as Father. The idea of God as our Father is a uniquely New Testament concept; it wasn't used in the Old Testament. Now Old Testament saints were saved in the same way that we are saved, except we look back to our Savior and Redeemer, crucified and risen. Old Testament saints looked to the future for a promised Savior and Redeemer who was to come. As Job, a contemporary of Abraham, said, "I know that my Redeemer lives" (Job 19:25). Going back to the beginning of the book of Genesis, they understood that there was a coming Savior. So the idea of God as Father was introduced by Jesus during His ministry on earth. And it's not found in the remainder of the book of Revelation.

Starting Revelation 4, we're off to the races. But before we start racing through Tribulation events in the text, we must consider two principles of interpretation for the events of the Tribulation throughout Revelation. The Tribulation account in the book of Revelation gives us an unclear picture, not a Google map. It would be nice if there was a nice clean timeline of these events. But the book of Revelation just does not work that way.

To help us understand the first principle, let's use the example of watching a movie in a theater. Imagine sitting in the theater, but instead of watching just one movie, you're watching two, on two different screens, one above the other. As you read through the book of Revelation, you'll notice that the visual images go back and forth, from scenes in Heaven to scenes on the earth. One scene is in Heaven, and then it shifts to earth, and then back and forth and back and forth.

It can be confusing as you read your way through this. Let's take a look at a few of these images and scenes that we see in Revelation:

> Then I saw in the right hand of him who sat on the throne a scroll with writing on both sides and sealed with seven seals. And I saw a mighty angel proclaiming in a loud voice, "Who is worthy to break the seals and open the scroll?" But no one in heaven or on earth or under the earth could open the scroll or even look inside it. I wept and wept because no one was found who was worthy to open the scroll or look inside. Then one of the elders said to me, "Do not weep! See, the Lion of the tribe of Judah, the Root of David, has triumphed. He is able to open the scroll and its seven seals." (Revelation 5:1–5)

If you've ever read about or listened to sermons based in the book of Revelation, you know God will pour out three series of judgments on the earth. These are the seal judgments, the trumpet judgments, and the bowl judgments. The seals being referred to here are not the cute creatures with flippers you might find along the coast. When you think of these seals, think of an ancient scroll that gets unrolled. The more you unroll, the more you're able to see what's written on the scroll. The scroll referred to here has seven seals. Think of a wax seal used in ancient times, in which a king or some other authority figure poured some hot wax on the edge of a scroll, in effect, sealing it. Then he would take his signet ring and stamp it into the hot wax. In that way, the recipient of that scroll, once it had been delivered, would know whether someone had tried to open it by breaking that seal to read its contents.

Back to our scene in Heaven. There is this seven-sealed scroll, and there is no one who is worthy, no one with the authority to break the seals and read the scroll. So there is a dilemma. John wept because no one was found worthy to open the scroll or to look inside it. "Then one of the elders said to me, 'Do not weep! See, the Lion of the tribe of Judah, the Root of David, has triumphed. He is able to open the scroll and its seven seals.'"

Jesus triumphed because He died on the cross to pay for our sins, and He rose from the dead. Jesus has triumphed over our sin! He has triumphed over death! He is the only one worthy to break these seals and open the scroll.

Now let's jump ahead to chapter 6 and a scene on the lower screen in the theater:

> I watched as he opened the sixth seal. There was a great
> earthquake. The sun turned black like sackcloth made
> of goat hair, the whole moon turned blood red, and the
> stars in the sky fell to earth, as figs drop from a fig tree
> when shaken by a strong wind. The heavens receded like
> a scroll being rolled up, and every mountain and island
> was removed from its place. (Revelation 6:12–14)

We're jumping into the middle of the seal judgments. This is describing earthquakes and pestilence and death, things like that. Some people will read, "The heavens receded like a scroll being rolled up, and every mountain and island was removed from its place," and say things like, "That's a nuclear bomb!" If you've ever seen a video of a nuclear bomb blowing up, with its big mushroom cloud, could this be a description of one going off? I would say it's possible, but I'm not ready to stake my life on it. It could simply be God opening His mouth and speaking it into existence!

There are all kinds of these images are seen throughout Revelation. Here's another example:

> And out of the smoke locusts came down on the earth and were given power like that of scorpions of the earth. ...The locusts looked like horses prepared for battle. On their heads they wore something like crowns of gold, and their faces resembled human faces. Their hair was like women's hair, and their teeth were like lions' teeth. They had breastplates like breastplates of iron, and the sound of their wings was like the thundering of many horses and chariots rushing into battle. They had tails with stingers, like scorpions, and in their tails they had power to torment people for five months. (Revelation 9:3, 7–10)

These things sound absolutely demonic! They've got scorpion tails with stingers and look extremely scary and weird. Some people might say this is a description of how John might try to understand military helicopters from his ancient perspective. You can play that kind of game and try to figure all that out, but ultimately, we just don't know. Is it possible John is describing military helicopters? Possibly. But again, these might be real demonic creatures! We just can't be dogmatic about such things.

Let's look at another scene, this one on the upper screen—the viewpoint of Heaven—and the lower screen—the earth's viewpoint—at the same time.

> After this I saw four angels standing at the four corners of the earth, holding back the four winds of

the earth to prevent any wind from blowing on the land or on the sea or on any tree. Then I saw another angel coming up from the east, having the seal of the living God. He called out in a loud voice to the four angels who had been given power to harm the land and the sea: "Do not harm the land or the sea or the trees until we put a seal on the foreheads of the servants of our God." Then I heard the number of those who were sealed:144,000 from all the tribes of Israel. (Revelation 7:1–4)

This is the opposite of the "mark of the beast," which the unsaved during the Tribulation will take. The seal of God will serve to protect these 144,000 from being harmed or killed by the Antichrist. There will be 12,000 from each of the twelve tribes of Israel, totaling 144,000. This will literally be 144,000 Jewish people who will have come to faith in Christ, and God will choose them and preserve them and give them this label. And God will protect them through the Tribulation. They will go into the world proclaiming the Gospel of the Kingdom. It will be the same message that Jesus was proclaiming when He came the first time. "The kingdom of God is at hand!" And it certainly will be near! They will be able to estimate just how near it is. This is the message that "will be preached in the whole world as a testimony to all nations" (Matthew 24:14). This will happen during the Tribulation, not during our time in the Church Age.

Great persecution will happen during this time. But these 144,000 will be protected. We see the 144,000 once more in Revelation 14:

Then I looked, and there before me was the Lamb, standing on Mount Zion, and with him 144,000 who had his name and his Father's name written on their foreheads. And I heard a sound from heaven like the roar of rushing waters and like a loud peal of thunder. The sound I heard was like that of harpists playing their harps. And they sang a new song before the throne and before the four living creatures and the elders. No one could learn the song except the 144,000 who had been redeemed from the earth. (Revelation 14:1–3)

Those will be some pretty powerful harps. Maybe they're electric guitars! The Greek word refers simply to stringed instruments. The setting is the end of the Tribulation, when Jesus (the Lamb) will stand on Mount Zion, which is a reference to Jerusalem. It might seem too early in Revelation for this to be the end of the Tribulation, but be patient. The timeline of Revelation is not linear. It doesn't just roll straight through. There isn't just a nice, neat sequence of events. The 144,000 will be there in that victorious moment to greet Jesus as He returns to the planet.

Back to the upper screen in chapter 7 of Revelation, to a scene in Heaven just before the end of the Tribulation:

> After this I looked, and there before me was a great multitude that no one could count, from every nation, tribe, people and language, standing before the throne and before the Lamb. They were wearing white robes and were holding palm branches in their hands. And they cried out in a loud voice: "Salvation belongs to our God, who sits on the throne, and to the Lamb." … Then one of the elders asked me, "These in white robes—who are they, and where did they come from?" I answered, "Sir, you know." And he said, "These are they who have come out of the great tribulation; they have washed their robes and made them white in the blood of the Lamb." (Revelation 7:9–10, 13–14)

This is a description of a great multitude, too numerous to count, of those who will be saved during the Tribulation and then be martyred or killed for their faith in Christ. And don't you know, that's exactly what's going to happen. The Church will be taken out of the way. There will be a crisis on the planet. The Antichrist will step into the void and find a way to calm everyone. There will be people who will pick up Bibles or watch videos of previous messages or Bible lessons on YouTube, or whatever will be around at that future time. And maybe they will say to themselves, "Maybe my absurd uncle Joe, who disappeared a few weeks ago, wasn't as off-point as I thought!" And they will take it seriously, put their faith in Jesus Christ, and spend some time getting ready for "that day" when Jesus will return.

CHAPTER 11

"LET'S GO SURFING NOW, EVERYBODY'S LEARNING HOW"

THE SEAL JUDGMENTS, THE TRUMPET judgments, and then the bowl judgments seemingly go from one right into the other. But they are not necessarily sequential. I mentioned in the previous chapter that they don't fit into a nice timeline. Let me try to explain that a little better. In Revelation chapter 8, we see the transition between the seal judgments and the trumpet judgments, which are revealed when the seventh seal is opened. The seven trumpet judges are angels with trumpets, and they all blow their trumpets. I'm hoping it will help us to understand the sequence of these events in the book of Revelation. It's hard to understand because our minds are linear. We automatically assume when we see a timeline of events that they take place one after the other, but the book of Revelation doesn't work that way.

I think most of us understand the concept of how waves work, especially waves during a rising tide. People who live on the coast of an ocean have to concern themselves with rising and falling tides. See if this makes sense. A wave comes to the shore and then recedes. Let's call that Wave 1. The tide is rising, so each subsequent wave crashes into the shore with greater volume and depth. Then the next wave, Wave 2, comes to the shore and then recedes. Then the third wave, Wave 3, crashes into the shore and then recedes. This is what's happening in the book of Revelation. The series of seal, trumpet, and bowl judgments land on the shore in three waves. Even within these waves, mini-waves occur. And the tide is rising, so each subsequent wave becomes more and more severe.

As you're reading through the book of Revelation, you have to understand these series of judgments as waves. When you get to the fifth, sixth, and seventh judgments in each series of judgments, you're getting pretty close to the coming of Christ in each series at that point. But then it recedes. And then another wave begins to rise. As it recedes, each wave, in a sense, goes back in time as well. It's almost like the phrase, "Three steps forward and one step back." You must take that into account as you read. As you get to the end of Revelation 16, just about all the judgments are done. Revelation 17 and 18 serve as a kind of addendum; they don't serve to advance the timeline. Understanding the concept of waves and rising tides helps us to understand how the timelines in the book of Revelation work.

Now, the book of Revelation also has some interesting characters. Two are found in Revelation 11:

> And I will appoint my two witnesses, and they will prophesy for 1,260 days, clothed in sackcloth." They are "the two olive trees" and the two lampstands, and "they stand before the Lord of the earth." If anyone tries to harm them, fire comes from their mouths and devours their enemies. This is how anyone who wants to harm them must die. They have power to shut up the heavens so that it will not rain during the time they are prophesying; and they have power to turn the waters into blood and to strike the earth with every kind of plague as often as they want. (Revelation 11:3–6)

The Tribulation is going to be seven years long; 1,260 days. Those seven years are then divided into two sets of three and a half years. There's a very significant event that happens at the midway point, which we talked about in chapter 8. That event is the abomination of desolation, that moment when the Antichrist will go into the Temple in Jerusalem and say, "Worship me." Everything will deteriorate from there; this is an understatement. But these two witnesses will be appointed for a specified time unknown to us. If anyone tries to harm them, fire will come from their mouths and devour their enemies. How cool is that? Fire-breathing prophets!

They will have the power to shut up the heavens so that they will not rain. It will not rain during the time they are prophesying. That is why some people propose a theory that these two prophets are Elijah and Moses because these were events that were happening during their ministries in the Old Testament. I don't know if this will be Elijah and Moses, but they will have power to turn the waters into blood and to strike the earth with every kind of plague as often as they want. They certainly will mirror, in some sense, the ministries of Elijah and Moses.

When they have finished their testimonies, when God says, "Time's up," the beast that will come up from the abyss will attack and overpower them. And kill them. God will allow the beast to do this as the two witnesses will have served their purposes.

> Now when they have finished their testimony, the beast that comes up from the Abyss will attack them, and overpower and kill them. Their bodies will lie in the public square of the great city—which is figuratively called Sodom and Egypt—where also their Lord was crucified. For three and a half days some from every people, tribe, language and nation will gaze on their bodies and refuse them burial. The inhabitants of the earth will gloat over them and will celebrate by sending each other gifts, because these two prophets had tormented those who live on the earth. But after the three and a half days the breath of life from God entered them, and they stood on their feet, and terror struck those who saw them. Then they heard a loud voice from heaven saying to them, "Come up here." And they went up to heaven in a cloud, while their enemies looked on. (Revelation 11:7–12)

After the two witnesses are killed, their bodies will lie on the public square of the great city, Jerusalem, which figuratively is called Sodom and Egypt. This is going to happen front and center in Jerusalem for three and a half days. People from every nation, every tribe, and every language will gaze at their bodies and not allow them to be buried. The inhabitants of the earth will gloat over them and celebrate by sending each other gifts. It's Christmastime for them! People will give each other gifts because these two guys are dead. Those who are the enemies of the Lord will cheer and celebrate and dance in the streets!

But after three and a half days of this nonsense, the breath of life from God will enter them. Now notice how much of the book of Revelation is written in the past tense. It is written in a way as if it already happened. It is future history. From God's perspective, these events have already happened. For us, we're still waiting to see what happens in the future, not what has happened in the past.

So these two witnesses stood on their feet and terror struck those who saw them. Then they heard a loud voice from Heaven saying, "Come up here." And they went up to Heaven in a cloud, while everyone just stood by and watched. What else could they do? That's awesome! And admittedly, it's weird too. But it will absolutely happen simply because God said so!

In chapters 13 and 14, there is a discussion of two beasts. These beasts are parts of a false or demonic trinity. As Christians, we understand that God exists as one God in three persons. We have Father, Son, and Holy Spirit. And as is typical for Satan because of his jealousy, he wants to copy or mimic everything about God. It shouldn't surprise us that he would want to present himself as a trinity. He will present himself to the earth as a false triad. The first beast is known as the Antichrist, a political world leader. The second beast is the false prophet, who will be some sort of religious leader. There will be a religious overtone to all that happens during the Tribulation.

> Then I saw a second beast, coming out of the earth. It had two horns like a lamb, but it spoke like a dragon. It exercised all the authority of the first beast on its behalf, and made the earth and its inhabitants worship the first beast, whose fatal wound had been healed. And it performed great signs, even causing fire to come down

from heaven to the earth in full view of the people. Because of the signs it was given power to perform on behalf of the first beast, it deceived the inhabitants of the earth. It ordered them to set up an image in honor of the beast who was wounded by the sword and yet lived. (Revelation 13:11–14)

At some point just before the middle point of the Tribulation, the Antichrist will be mortally wounded in his head; perhaps he will be shot in the head. Everyone will think he has died. The second beast, the false prophet, will come in and perform some sort of pseudo-miracle that will allow the Antichrist to seemingly rise from the dead.

At that point, the false prophet will point to the Antichrist as the one the world must worship, giving his stamp of approval.

The second beast was given power to give breath to the image of the first beast, so that the image could speak and cause all who refused to worship the image to be killed. It also forced all people, great and small, rich and poor, free and slave, to receive a mark on their right hands or on their foreheads, so that they could not buy or sell unless they had the mark, which is the name of the beast or the number of its name. (Revelation 13:15–17)

In other words, there will be a statue of some sort that will represent the Antichrist set up in the Temple in Jerusalem. The people will be forced to worship this image, this idol. This image or idol will be able to speak. Walt Disney studios will have nothing on what this will end up looking like and how it will operate. The way Disney is headed, they might be the ones employed to make it happen. If you've ever seen the Hall of Presidents or any other attraction with animatronic characters at Disney World, you'll know what is meant by that.

People will either worship this beast, this imitator of God, or be killed. Period. Talk about having to get off the fence, right? Here in the United States of America, we have created a generation of cultural

Christians who love to ride the fence. "Am I in, or am I out? Am I a Christian or not?" Well, on Sunday, some people act like they are Christians. But Monday through Saturday, they'll do their own things, living for themselves and not for the Lord. But during the Tribulation, people will be confronted with a stark choice. No pretending. No faking it. Either you are in, or you are out.

If you choose to trust and follow Christ, you will have to run for your life and go into hiding or you will be captured, imprisoned, and eventually killed for your faith in Christ. It's that simple. If you are out, if you choose to take the easy way by following the Antichrist and be "safe" by denying the Lord Jesus, it will mean you are lost and destined for hell. This decision will force all people—great and small, rich and poor, free and slave—to receive a mark on their right hands or on foreheads. Here we go—this is it—the mark of the beast. You've probably heard about this. People will not be able to buy or sell unless they have this mark on their hands or on their foreheads.

If people don't have the mark of the beast, they will not be able to gas up the vehicle. No trips to Walmart because when they go into Walmart, someone will be there to make sure that they have that image on their hands or foreheads. It may be when a person walks in or when they check out. It will be similar to what already happens at a Sam's Club or Costco. It will all be enforced by government police or military. But anyone willing to get this mark of the beast is not a Christian. It would mean they don't belong to the Lord. And that's not a good place to be!

John writes, "This calls for wisdom. Let the person who has insight calculate the number of the beast, for it is the number of a man. That number is 666" (Revelation 13:18). What is the number of man? The number of man is six. It is imperfect. The number of God is seven. Seven is the number of perfection. The number of man is incomplete, imperfect. It is the number of humankind because without God, we are incomplete and imperfect. That's a description of us. There are three of the beasts having to do with the false trinity. Three sixes, then, are the numbers of imperfection tied together. They represent the beast. Understand that nobody will be tricked into taking the mark of the beast. It will be obvious. It will be blunt. It will be clear. They will have to choose one way or the other.

As we mentioned before, Revelation 17–18 lie outside the timeline. Both chapters describe the destruction of what is known as "Mystery Babylon." Babylon is an ancient city of the Chaldeans located in modern-day Iraq. This city is the place of origin for several false religions. It was the center of commerce in its day when Nebuchadnezzar, the emperor of Babylon, was a big deal. Chapter 17 deals with the false religion of Babylon. Chapter 18 deals with the political rule of Babylon. Both will be destroyed.

> One of the seven angels who had the seven bowls came and said to me, "Come, I will show you the punishment of the great prostitute, who sits by many waters. With her the kings of the earth committed adultery, and the inhabitants of the earth were intoxicated with the wine of her adulteries." (Revelation 17:1–2)

Some of the scenes in the book of Revelation contain images that would qualify for an R-rating because of how gruesome they are. It also uses metaphors for sexually explicit and immoral behaviors. The great city is depicted as a prostitute who commits adultery with the kings of the earth. The sin of adultery used here is a familiar metaphor for the sin of idolatry. The sin of adultery was used several times in the Old Testament to describe idolatry. In the book of Hosea, God used the prophet's relationship with his wife, who was an adulterous prostitute, to illustrate the unfaithfulness of Israel, who often went "a whoring" (KJV) or chasing after false gods. God viewed the Israelites chasing after false gods as a form of prostitution.

The way this woman in Revelation 17 is described is quite horrible:

> The name written on her forehead was a mystery: *Babylon the great the mother of prostitutes and of the abominations of the earth.* I saw that the woman was drunk with the blood of God's holy people, the blood of those who

bore testimony to Jesus. When I saw her, I was greatly astonished. (Revelation 17:5–6; italics added)

The Old Testament has much information about Babylon as the source of false religion, going back to Genesis 10–11, which is the account of the building of the tower of Babel. Babylon was not only important politically but was also important in a religious sense. Nimrod, who was the founder of Babylon, had a wife named Semiramis, who founded the secret religious rites of the Babylonian mysteries. These mystery religions were forced to shut down under the Persians in the prophet Daniel's day. The Babylonian cultists eventually moved to Pergamum, where one of the seven churches in Revelation was located. These false religious leaders later moved on to Rome, where they were influential in paganizing Christianity several hundred years after the resurrection of Christ. Babylon, then, represents the symbol of apostasy—false religion—and the blasphemous substitution of idol worship for the true worship of God in Christ. In Revelation 17–18, we read of Babylon receiving its final judgment.[1]

---

[1] John F. Walvoord, *The Bible Knowledge Commentary: New Testament Edition*, John F. Walvoord and Roy B. Zuck, eds. (Wheaton, IL: Victor Books, 1983), 970.

CHAPTER 12

DON'T FORGET THE MAIN THING

As you make your way through the book of Revelation, it might be easy to get bogged down by all the imagery and confusing text. Hopefully, some of the principles we've talked about will help you to get a better grasp on this last New Testament book. Still, there is much in the book of Revelation that we just won't understand. But we must not forget to let the main thing be the main thing. The theme of the book of Revelation, the major point of the book, is the person of Jesus Christ, His coming and making things right. Think about all that is wrong in the world. How many of you in the last few years have complained about all the wrong that is going on in the world today?

When Jesus comes, praise the Lord, He will set all the wrongs in the world right. Revelation 16 shows two views of that. The judgment and wrath of God are hard for us to comprehend or to look at. The first view is from those who had been declared righteous, who had trusted in Christ as Savior, and who had gotten saved during the Tribulation.

> Then I heard the angel in charge of the waters say: "You are just in these judgments, O Holy One, you who are and who were; for they have shed the blood of your holy people and your prophets, and you have given them blood to drink as they deserve." And I heard the altar

respond: "Yes, Lord God Almighty, true and just are your judgments." (Revelation 16:5–7)

Their view of God's wrath being poured out is, "Lord, you are right in these judgments. You are just in pouring out this wrath. You are true in your judgments." This is God's justice according to what He deems is right and true.

This next part is hard for us to read. You see this in several places in the book of Revelation, but we don't want to imagine this part:

> People gnawed their tongues in agony and cursed the God of heaven because of their pains and their sores, *but they refused to repent of what they had done.* (Revelation 16:10b–11; italics added)

> From the sky huge hailstones, each weighing about a hundred pounds, fell on people. And *they cursed God* on account of the plague of hail, because the plague was so terrible. (Revelation 16:21; italics added)

Notice the italicized phrases. They refused to repent of what they had done. They cursed God—instead of repenting—because of His wrath. These judgments that God will pour out will be horrific. And the people who are on the receiving end of them will know where this wrath is coming from. They will know that it is coming from the hand of God. And yet God, even at this point, is giving them an opportunity to repent because that is the mercy and the heart of God.

God loves you so much that He sent His Son to die on the cross for you. He sacrificed His own Son, Jesus, who willingly went to the cross. Jesus didn't deserve that. They beat Him. They whipped Him. They spit at Him. They plucked His beard. They put a crown of thorns on His head. They nailed Him to a cross. He shed His blood, and He died for you. That's how much He loves you. And His mercy is so great. He is not willing that any should perish, but that all should come to repentance. Even to the end of the Tribulation.

That has been God's story throughout history. Before God flooded the earth back in Noah's day, what was Noah's responsibility besides building the ark? He was proclaiming, "Hey guys, the rain is coming! A flood is coming! Don't you want to join me? Don't you want to repent?" But no one did. Only Noah and his family were saved on the ark. The opportunity was given for the people to repent, but they chose not to. The Lord told Jonah to go to Nineveh, which was a wicked Gentile city where the people did wicked things to others. Jonah didn't want to go there because he knew God's mercy was so great and so wonderful that the people of Nineveh might repent. Jonah didn't want that to happen, but that was the heart of God for the people of Nineveh. At the end of the book of Jonah, the people of Nineveh did repent, but Jonah sat outside the city, got depressed, and pitied himself. And even here, during the Tribulation, the people will refuse to repent in the face of terrible wrath and judgment. They will be given opportunity after opportunity after opportunity to repent. Yet they will refuse.

When Jesus finally returns, what is foretold in Philippians 2:10–11 will finally come to pass: "At the name of Jesus every knee should bow, in heaven and on earth and under the earth, and every tongue acknowledge that Jesus Christ is Lord, to the glory of God the Father." Let's state the obvious here. Wouldn't it be so much better to do that now? Wouldn't it be so much better to willingly bow your heart, to bow your life before the Lord and say, "Lord, I repent of my sin. I repent of my selfishness. I repent of my trying to do it my way, of trying to be my own God. And I trust you. I trust you with my life." It's more than just mental acknowledgment. It is bowing your heart and your will to God and trusting in His grace and goodness. It is saying, "I believe that Jesus died on that cross, was buried, and rose again from the dead. I now trust you with my life. I put my life in your hands. There's no plan B. My life is yours; I trust you with it."

Have you done that? Have you made that conscious decision? It's not about, "I was raised in a Christian family, so I must be a Christian." It's not about, "I've gone to church all this time, so I must be a Christian." No! That's not how anyone is saved. We're saved when we make the decision in our hearts and our wills, and say, "Lord, I give You my life. I trust You with it. It belongs to You. I trust You." If not today, then in the future, you need to make a decision. Don't put it off! Don't wait too long. Nobody knows how long it will be before they die or when the Rapture will happen. But make no mistake about it. When Jesus returns, you and everyone else will have to bow, and with your tongue, you will acknowledge that Jesus Christ is Lord and King! If you refuse to repent and trust Him now in this life, you will be bowing and gnawing at your tongue in agony and pain, cursing God the whole time, and eventually end up in hell. That is the choice that you must make.

There will be no one in hell saying, "Oh, I wanted to get saved. I really did. I just didn't have an opportunity." That's not going to happen. They will be there of their own choice. We trust in a sovereign God, who has given us the opportunity to repent and to trust Him. Even those who have never heard the name of Jesus have already rejected what revelation they have been given in creation and have chosen to worship themselves or the creation around them. And so I ask you, have you trusted the Lord Jesus Christ? Have you trusted Him? Have you trusted Him as Lord and Savior of your life? His return is imminent! I beg you, don't delay!

SECTION 5

THE END OF
THE STORY

CHAPTER 13

THE ACTUAL RETURN
AND THE KINGDOM

W<small>HEN WE TALK ABOUT THE</small> Second Coming of Jesus, there are two things in view. Let's try to explain it by referring to another event we look forward to each year—Christmas. This may sound odd, but follow me here. Do you look forward to Christmas? Now, when I ask that, are you saying that you look forward to the season of Christmas, whenever that may begin for you? Maybe you begin decorating really early, like as soon as the calendar turns to November. Others perhaps wait until at least the day after Thanksgiving. Others wait until the beginning of December. It's the whole season of Christmas that most people look forward to.

And then *maybe* some would say they really look forward to the actual day of Christmas, just the day itself. Not all the stuff that goes beforehand, just the day of Christmas. Nothing else. When the Second Coming of Christ is mentioned, we have to ask, "Are you referring to all the events associated with the Second Coming or just the actual day of Christ's Second Coming?" The Second Coming of Christ can refer to all the events that surround His Second Coming, beginning with the Rapture of the Church, the Tribulation, His actual coming, and then the beginning of the Millennial Kingdom. The Second Coming of Christ can refer to all of that.

The same is true of the phrase, "the Day of the Lord," or, "that Day." It can refer to all those events, or it can specifically refer to that one day when Jesus will split the sky open, step back in from eternity, and set His foot down in Jerusalem. His actual return. In this chapter, we're talking about that specific day, the actual moment in time when Jesus will set His foot back on the planet. Revelation 19:11 begins our discussion:

> I saw heaven standing open and there before me was a white horse, whose rider is called Faithful and True. With justice he judges and wages war. His eyes are like blazing fire, and on his head are many crowns. He has a name written on him that no one knows but he himself. He is dressed in a robe dipped in blood, and his name is the Word of God. The armies of heaven were following him, riding on white horses and dressed in fine linen, white and clean. Coming out of his mouth is a sharp sword with which to strike down the nations. "He will rule them with an iron scepter." He treads the winepress of the fury of the wrath of God Almighty. On his robe and on his thigh he has this name written: KING OF KINGS AND LORD OF LORDS. (Revelation 19:11–16)

When Jesus comes, He will come riding a white horse. His eyes will be like blazing fire. I don't think anyone will want to look directly at Jesus at this moment. The many crowns represent that Jesus is the King of Kings. The name written on Him that no one knows is perhaps a heavenly language that no one has ever heard before. Jesus will be wearing a robe dipped in blood, a reference to how He is worthy because of His sacrifice when he shed His blood on the cross. The armies of Heaven will be following Him. Guess who's going to be in His army at His Second Coming? That's right. It will be us, the Church Age saints. We can't imagine what that day will be like. But we'll all be dressed in fine white linen, which speaks to the righteousness that we have, not of our own accord, but because Christ's righteousness has been accredited to us. The sword from Jesus's mouth represents a stylistic way of saying that when Jesus speaks, death and destruction will happen. Jesus will defeat His enemies with just the spoken word!

So here we are. This is *the* event. It will be glorious when we see Jesus bring His righteousness to pass on the earth. There will be devastation and destruction and wrath. We will be like heavenly cheerleaders. It's not like we're going to be riding horses with swords swinging or guns blazing. We will be an army of praisers. We'll be shouting the Lord's praise at the top of our lungs. There will be a battle, but it sounds a little anticlimactic. It doesn't seem like it's going to be much of a battle. Jesus will speak, and the unbelievers of that age will be destroyed. That's pretty much it.

Then several judgments will take place, particularly of Jews. We looked at those back in Matthew 25. These judgments will usher in the Kingdom of God. This is referenced in both the Old and New Testaments. It is called the Kingdom of God, or the Millennial Kingdom. The word "millennium" means one thousand. So the Millennial Kingdom will last for a thousand years. Some people question this. Will it be a thousand literal years, or was this a way to say a long time? Because of the way the number is repeated in chapter 20, there's no reason to believe that we shouldn't take its meaning to be literal.

Jesus will reign on the earth for a thousand years as was His promise going back to the Old Testament.

> And I saw an angel coming down out of heaven, having the key to the Abyss and holding in his hand a great chain. He seized the dragon, that ancient serpent, who is the devil, or Satan, and bound him for a thousand years. He threw him into the Abyss, and locked and sealed it over him, to keep him from deceiving the nations anymore until the thousand years were ended. After that, he must be set free for a short time. (Revelation 20:1–3)

This kicks off the Millennial Kingdom. An angel will take the dragon (Satan), bind him, and throw him into the abyss, where he will be held for a thousand years. But Satan has one more role to play before his final demise. We'll see that in a little bit.

Here's an interesting question: What will life be like on the earth when, for a thousand years, there will be no influence from Satan or any of his network of demons? They all will be gone during the Millennial Kingdom. Can you imagine? No, we really can't. Another trademark of the Millennial Kingdom is that it will be a time of incredible peace like we have never seen before. We don't even know what this is like. The animal kingdom will be completely different. How we relate to the world will be completely different. How we relate to each other, and how we relate to the Lord will be completely different. Throughout the Old Testament, particularly in the prophetic books, we get little pictures of what living conditions will be like on the planet during this time. Look at Isaiah 11:

> The wolf will live with the lamb, the leopard will lie down with the goat, the calf and the lion and the yearling together; and a little child will lead them. The cow will feed with the bear, their young will lie down together, and the lion will eat straw like the ox. The infant will play near the cobra's den, the young child will put its hand into the viper's nest. They will neither harm nor destroy on all my holy mountain, for the earth will be filled with the knowledge of the Lord as the waters cover the sea. (Isaiah 11:6–9)

Here we see that with the ushering in of the Millennial Kingdom, the animals will revert to their original design and creation from before the Fall in the garden of Eden. Wolves will no longer hunt and feed on lambs. You may occasionally see pictures of a wolf cuddling with a lamb. The fear of humankind that the Fall (Adam and Eve's original sin and its consequences on the creation) instilled in animals will not exist. They will be able to approach us just like a domesticated animal would approach us. And you'll be able to wrestle with a tiger and frolic with a panda. You'll be able to go swimming with dolphins and sharks. You'll be able to lie down with a lion and give his mane a good petting. "The cow will feed with the bear, their young will lie down together, and the lion will eat straw like the ox." I don't know how that's going to work because we've seen too many nature documentaries of lions chasing down these poor zebras and gazelles and eating them. But that won't happen during the Millennial Kingdom. Still, I just can't imagine a lion sitting there chewing its cud or eating hay and being happy about it.

Let's step back for a moment and talk about how people will eat during the Millennial Kingdom. Remember, our relationship with animals will be different. The idea of us eating meat during the Millennial Kingdom will probably not happen. My guess is that we'll probably not be eating steaks or fried chicken during the Millennium. Now if that disappoints you, you're missing the point. If a lion will be satisfied eating hay, I think we'll be satisfied eating a vegetarian diet. Remember, we Church Age saints as well as Old Testament saints and Tribulation saints will be ruling with Christ on earth in resurrected bodies. Whether we will even need to eat is unknown. But I think we will eat. It will still be a source of joy and fellowship during this time for resurrected saints. But it won't be because we will need food for sustenance.

For those who survive the Tribulation as believers, they will go into the Millennial Kingdom with their regular bodies. They will marry and have children and families. There will be grandchildren and great-grandchildren and so on. How long will they live? Maybe they will go back to the early book of Genesis times, when people lived for hundreds of years. There will be no famine, no disease, no war. None of those terrible things will occur during the Kingdom.

> Never again will there be in it an infant who lives but a few days, or an old man who does not live out his years; the one who dies at a hundred will be thought a mere child; the one who fails to reach a hundred will be considered accursed. (Isaiah 65:20)

And the reason a man may die at a hundred years old is because of his wickedness. Now that may sound odd during the Millennial Kingdom. You might think, *Wait a minute. I thought the devil and his angels will be locked up in the abyss. How will it be possible for a man to be considered accursed or wicked?* The reality is that all those people who go into the Millennial Kingdom (not those with resurrected bodies)

103

will be marrying and having children and carrying on with their lives. They will continue with their sinful natures. All their children and grandchildren and so on will also have to choose to trust in Jesus Christ as their Savior during the Kingdom. They will have to choose, "Am I going to honor Christ? Am I going to live for Christ?" There will be many who will say, "I'm just going to go through the motions." They will have to openly bow to Christ during this time because everybody will bow to Christ during the Kingdom. Some will bow their hearts and their wills as well. Some will just do it because that's what everyone else is doing. They will bow because they feel like they *have to* do it. That attitude will play a role in what Satan does at the end of the Millennial Kingdom. Stay tuned.

Take a look at the last statement from Isaiah 11:9: "The earth will be filled with the knowledge of the Lord as the waters cover the sea." How much do the waters cover the sea? Yeah, completely, all the way. And that's what it will be like on the planet. During the time of the Millennial Kingdom, there won't be a need for evangelism. No one will come across someone who hasn't heard of the Lord. It just won't happen. Everyone will know the Lord.

It will also be a time for justice:

> I saw thrones on which were seated those who had been given authority to judge. And I saw the souls of those who had been beheaded because of their testimony about Jesus and because of the word of God. They had not worshiped the beast or its image and had not received its mark on their foreheads or their hands. They came to life and reigned with Christ a thousand years. (Revelation 20:4)

Those who will be given authority to judge will include Church Age saints, Old Testament saints, and those believers who will be martyred during the Tribulation. We will all be ruling and reigning with Christ.

The next two verses speak of the two major resurrections that will occur during the End Times:

(The rest of the dead did not come to life until the thousand years were ended.) This is the first resurrection. Blessed and holy are those who share in the first resurrection. The second death has no power over them, but they will be priests of God and of Christ and will reign with him for a thousand years. (Revelation 20:5–6)

Just as there is a first and a second death, there will also be a first and a second resurrection. You won't want to be a part of the second death or the second resurrection. You'll only want to go through the first ones. The first resurrection will be for believers and will happen at different times. Jesus was the firstfruits of the first resurrection. The Rapture will serve as the next part of the first resurrection. More will be resurrected at the end of the Tribulation (Old Testament saints and Tribulation martyrs). These are all part of the first resurrection and will not experience the second death. The second resurrection will take place at the end of the Millennial Kingdom and is reserved for all the lost dead of all ages. If you are lost and without Christ, this is when you will be resurrected. Those who will be at this resurrection will experience the second death. We'll look at what happens to them in the next chapter.

CHAPTER 14

THE GREAT WHITE THRONE AND THE ETERNAL STATE

At the end of the Millennial Kingdom there will be one final battle. There have been hints of this battle up to this point.

> When the thousand years are over, Satan will be released from his prison and will go out to deceive the nations in the four corners of the earth—Gog and Magog—and to gather them for battle. In number they are like the sand on the seashore. They marched across the breadth of the earth and surrounded the camp of God's people, the city he loves. But fire came down from heaven and devoured them. (Revelation 20:7–9)

Why does the Lord give Satan one more go around? Wasn't the first one bad enough? There is a reason why. Can you imagine how many people there will be on the planet during a thousand years of very minimal death, no war, no famine, and no disease? The earth will be so full of people. And many of those people will be lost, even in perfect conditions with no opportunities to outwardly sin. At that point, Satan will be set loose, and he will gather all the lost people for battle. Their number will be like the sand on the seashore. There will be multitudes and millions of people who will be lost and ready to rebel against the Lord on the throne. They will choose to follow Satan, that great deceiver, instead.

But it won't be for very long. They will march against Jerusalem, but fire will come down from heaven and devour them. That's it! *Boom*. Not much of a battle there. Although they will have the ability to read the Scriptures and see the Lord in action for a thousand years, they will still choose to follow the devil and rebel against God. That just emphasizes the point of our wicked human natures. Even without temptation and the influence of the devil and his cohorts for a thousand years, so many people, when given the opportunity, will choose evil and sin and rebel against the righteous, holy, loving, and merciful God. They will freely choose to go to war against the Lord.

And so ends the final battle at the end of the Millennial Kingdom. Now we are introduced to something called the "lake of fire," or the, "lake of burning sulfur."

> And the devil, who deceived them, was thrown into the lake of burning sulfur, where the beast and the false prophet had been thrown. They will be tormented day and night for ever and ever. (Revelation 20:10)

And then there will be the final judgment. This final judgment is known as the Great White Throne Judgment. Thankfully, we Christians and any of the Old Testament saints will not have to face this judgment. For people who find themselves at the Great White Throne Judgment, it's not going to be a good day because they will spend an eternity apart from God in a place called the lake of fire, where "they will be tormented day and night for ever and ever."

Here is what the Great White Throne Judgment will look like:

> Then I saw a great white throne and him who was seated on it. The earth and the heavens fled from his presence, and there was no place for them. And I saw the dead, great and small, standing before the throne, and books were opened. Another book was opened, which is the book of life. The dead were judged according to what they had done as recorded in the books. The sea gave up the dead that were in it, and death and Hades gave

up the dead that were in them, and each person was judged according to what they had done. Then death and Hades were thrown into the lake of fire. The lake of fire is the second death. Anyone whose name was not found written in the book of life was thrown into the lake of fire. (Revelation 20:11–15)

All those lost people from every age will find themselves standing before the Lord. All their sins will have been recorded in these books. They will have to account for all their sins. And, of course, no one will be able to give an account for any of their sins. One collection of books will contain all their sinful acts, their wicked deeds, during their lifetimes. Then another separate book, the Book of Life, will be opened. But their names will not be found there. It will be determined that they never trusted Jesus Christ with their lives. Instead, they trusted in themselves. And it will be the end for them. They will then be thrown into the lake of fire, which is eternal.

Now, for those of us who are believers, we will not be judged based on our works. Thankfully, we have the Advocate, the Lord Jesus. We will not have to stand before the Lord to be judged for our sins because they were accounted for and paid for at the cross. When Jesus died on the cross, He paid for our sins. They were judged there on the cross. That's the essence of the Good News. Both judgments are based on works, but for believers, it won't be our sins being judged because Jesus took those sins with Him to the cross.

That leads us to the final part of the story, the eternal state, "the new heaven and the new earth." This is what we normally think of when we talk about Heaven. Whatever you've heard about the glories of Heaven, much of it has been anecdotes. Streets of gold and gates of pearl, that kind of thing. We think of angels floating on clouds, strumming harps. Sometimes people talk about their loved ones becoming angels or gaining wings when they die. That is not a correct idea of Heaven. We will still be people in Heaven. When the Scriptures talk about, "the heavens and the earth," that's not a reference to the heavens as being God's residence. Rather, it's referring to the skies, stars, and the universe. At the end of all things, God will make a new heaven and a new earth. We get to start over if you will.

When it comes to understanding Heaven, here's the main point to understand. Heaven will not be about the landscape, the opulence, the stuff that will be there. It will be about relationship. The language of relationship is essential in any discussion of Heaven. It won't be about streets of gold or whether we get to eat meat. It won't be about getting to do this or that. It's about relationship.

> Then I saw "a new heaven and a new earth," for the first heaven and the first earth had passed away, and there was no longer any sea. I saw the Holy City, the new Jerusalem, coming down out of heaven from God, prepared as a bride beautifully dressed for her husband. And I heard a loud voice from the throne saying, "Look! God's dwelling place is now among the people, and he will dwell with them. They will be his people, and God himself will be with them and be their God. 'He will wipe every tear from their eyes. There will be no more death' or mourning or crying or pain, for the old order of things has passed away." (Revelation 21:1–4)

There will be, "a new heaven and a new earth." Again, this is not a reference to God's residence in Heaven but a reference to the moon, stars, and universe. There will no longer be big expanses of oceans like we currently have. There will still be bodies of water, but no more oceans. And then the Holy City, New Jerusalem, will descend to the earth. This basically means that Heaven and earth will merge. God will dwell with us on the earth. It will literally be Heaven on earth.

"God himself will be with them and be their God." God will dwell with us in this new paradise of Heaven on earth. We will belong to God, and He will belong to us. We will live in relationship with the Lord unhindered by sin, unhindered by any kind of evil thought or wrong motive. We can't even comprehend what that will be like. And God will wipe every tear from our eyes. There will be no more death or mourning or crying or pain because the old order of things will have passed away. And again, that speaks to relationship with each other. All the things that we pass through in this life that bring tears and pain and sorrow and mourning will be gone in Heaven: "He who was seated on the throne said, 'I am making everything new!' Then he said, 'Write this down, for these words are trustworthy and true'" (Revelation 21:5).

I don't know what the rest of this earthly existence has in store for each of us. But I know on that day we will be able to gather and remember the coming of this day. And this day is coming as sure as Jesus is risen from the dead and is alive today! His promise is true. We will find ourselves at this moment. Absolutely. Just as sure as you are sitting where you are right now, reading this book, this wonderful day is coming. I can't wait. I can't wait to see my Savior's face. And all that makes up this present life and world will be past tense and done. All the sin and pain and sorrow we see in our world will be gone. And when Jesus said, "Write this down for these words are trustworthy and true," it's as if the Lord is saying, "This is going to happen. It's a done deal." This is what's coming, and I can't wait!

Jesus said in John 16:33, "I have told you these things, so that in me you may have peace. In this world, you will have trouble. But take heart! I have overcome the world." When we put our trust in Jesus, we're just grabbing on to Him and holding on for dear life. The good news is that Jesus holds on to us, and He will never let us go!

> He said to me: "It is done. I am the Alpha and the Omega, the Beginning and the End. To the thirsty I will give water without cost from the spring of the water of life. Those who are victorious will inherit all this, and I will be their God and they will be my children. But the cowardly, the unbelieving, the vile, the murderers, the sexually immoral, those who practice magic arts, the idolaters and all liars—they will be consigned to the fiery lake of burning sulfur. This is the second death." (Revelation 21:6–8)

Those who are victorious, those who overcome will inherit all this. It won't be because of anything we have done. It's all because of Jesus. We'll just be riding His coattails.

The word for "children" at the end of verse 7 describes an adopted son who is old enough to recognize what he is receiving from the relationship with his Father. Because we have been adopted into the family, we receive the inheritance and the blessings, all the privileges that come out of that relationship with the Father. And then, as you read the list in verse 8 concerning those who will be consigned to the lake of fire, remember that this is a list for those who are without Christ. They will face the Lord at the great white throne judgment and have to answer for their sins. But for those who are in Christ, we will not be judged based on our works, praise the Lord! Jesus took our judgment upon Himself on the cross.

CHAPTER 15

HOW SHOULD WE RESPOND?

As we come to the close of this book, let's look at a few application points as we consider all that we have covered concerning the Second Coming of Jesus.

WE SHOULD MAKE PLANS AS IF JESUS ISN'T COMING BACK FOR A THOUSAND YEARS

Absolutely. You invest. You save. You raise your family. Be faithful in supporting and serving your local church. Be generous to those in need. You plan for retirement. You do all of it.

> Whatever you do, work at it with all your heart, as working for the Lord, not for human masters, since you know that you will receive an inheritance from the Lord as a reward. It is the Lord Christ you are serving. (Colossians 3:23–24)

You serve and plan and raise your family as if Jesus is not coming back anytime soon. But ...

AT THE SAME TIME, LIVE YOUR LIFE AS IF JESUS COULD RETURN AT ANY MOMENT

This is not a contradiction. It is simply true. Jesus could come for His Church at any moment. It is the doctrine of the imminency of Christ's return. Peter writes about how we should live in light of Christ's return:

> But the day of the Lord will come like a thief. The heavens will disappear with a roar; the elements will be destroyed by fire, and the earth and everything done in it will be laid bare. Since everything will be destroyed in this way, *what kind of people ought you to be? You ought to live holy and godly lives as you look forward to the day of God* and speed its coming. That day will bring about the destruction of the heavens by fire, and the elements will melt in the heat. But in keeping with his promise we are looking forward to a new heaven and a new earth, where righteousness dwells. So then, dear friends, *since you are looking forward to this, make every effort to be found spotless, blameless and at peace with him.* (2 Peter 3:10–14; italics added)

Note the italicized phrases. That's what all of this is about. All our discussions about the Second Coming of Jesus should lead to living holy and godly lives, to making every effort to be found spotless, blameless, and at peace with the Lord.

FINALLY, ASK AND ANSWER THIS QUESTION: "AM I IN THE FAITH?"

The apostle Paul put it this way:

> Examine yourselves to see whether you are in the faith; test yourselves. Do you not realize that Christ Jesus is in you—unless, of course, you fail the test? And I trust

that you will discover that we have not failed the test.
(2 Corinthians 13:5–6)

If there's one thing our study of the Second Coming of Jesus ought to settle in our hearts, it is this question. "Am I in Him? Am I in Christ? Have I trusted Jesus Christ as my Lord and Savior? Have I made peace with Him?" He's already done all the work. All the peacekeeping work has been done. Jesus accomplished it all at the cross. All we must do is believe. All we must do is accept it. My prayer is if you have not already done so, trust in Jesus Christ with your very life and that you would make that decision today. Do not delay for it could cost you everything!

STUDY GUIDE

There are several ways to take advantage of this study guide. First, you can use it as a personal Bible study resource. You can work through the questions after reading each chapter, or you could work through the guide after reading the complete book. Second, a small group could work through the study guide chapter by chapter, which would provide a fifteen-week study. Or you could be more selective in choosing which questions to use and study the book section by section (three chapters per section), which would provide for a five-week study. However you decide to use this study guide, the hope is you will benefit from your further study of this topic.

If as you use this study guide you have questions about an individual question or about anything in the book, please feel free to email me at: dailyintheword@yahoo.com. I will attempt to respond to questions there.

SECTION 1
LAYING THE GROUNDWORK

Chapter 1: Hacking through the Deep Weeds

1. Why does it seem like every time there is some sort of national or world crisis, Christians start thinking about the Second Coming?

2. Read Matthew 24:4–8, Luke 21:11, and 1 Thessalonians 5:1–3. How would you answer the question, "Are current events pointing to a soon return of Jesus?" Why did you answer this way?

3. Were you disappointed to read the author's answer to that question? Why or why not? Did his answer contradict your previous view on the subject?

4. What was your response to the history given in chapter 1 to demonstrate that perhaps we are <u>not</u> currently facing a unique time in history?

5. If someone were to ask you, "Why does God allow evil in the world?" how would you answer? What kinds of evil in the world sometimes makes you question if God is really in control of everything?

Chapter 2: Jesus *Is* Coming Again

1. Do you really believe that Jesus Christ is coming again? What are some things that make people hesitate to believe it? What makes you hesitate—if you do—to believe it?

2. Read Revelation 1:1–3. The word "revelation" means "a peeling back," "a revealing," "an unveiling of something that was hidden." Who and what will be unveiled by the revelation given to John?

3. John states that we will be blessed if we read and hear his message and take it to heart (Revelation 1:3). In what ways do you think he expects us to take this message to heart?

4. What do you think of the statement: There is nothing more in biblical prophecy that must happen before the Rapture of the Church? This statement speaks to the imminency of Christ's return for His Church. Define the word "imminent."

5. Read Matthew 24:36 and Luke 12:46. Is it hard to accept that these two passages do not concern the Rapture of the Church? What are they concerned with?

Chapter 3: Precautions When Reading Prophecy

1. Read Matthew 24:40–42. What is the consequence for reading this passage out of context? How does understanding the context of a passage help us not to make assumptions about what a passage might mean?

2. Read 1 Thessalonians 4:16–5:3. Take special note of the pronouns used; see chapter 3 of this book. How does understanding the use of language and grammar help us to understand who a particular passage is addressing?

3. Read Revelation 1:7–8. Does this passage deal with Church Age believers, or does it deal with Israel? Now read Zechariah 12:10. How does checking the references found in the Bible help you to determine the meaning of Scripture?

4. Often the proper understanding of Scripture is given in the context of warnings about misleading, greedy, or immoral teachers. How could these kinds of false teachers lead you down a dangerous path concerning the subject of the End Times?

5. Read 2 Timothy 3:16–17. What implications does this passage have for you regarding your study of the book of Revelation and other End Times Scriptures and their application to your life? Why do you think Paul stresses the importance of Scripture in the context of warnings about misleading, immoral teachers?

SECTION 2
THE RAPTURE AND MORE

Chapter 4: Understanding the Rapture

1. Why do you think so many people are fascinated with knowing future prophecy—biblical or otherwise? Why do you think God has not told us when it might occur?

2. Read 1 Thessalonians 4:13–18. What sequence of events does Paul say will occur when Christ comes for His Church? How would Paul's words have been an encouragement to the Thessalonians? How are they an encouragement to us?

3. Paul indicates that when a Christian dies, his body "sleeps" until Christ returns to for His Church. This raises the question: Where does the Christian's spirit (the person) go when this happens? Read 2 Corinthians 5:8 and Philippians 1:23–24 and summarize what you read there.

4. Read Revelation 19:11–15. What differences do you notice between the events described here and in 1 Thessalonians 4:13–18?

5. If the Rapture were to occur in your lifetime, what would you like to accomplish before that event? In what condition would you like God to find your relationship with Him? Your relationships with family or friends? Your work?

Chapter 5: Other Perspectives of the Rapture

1. Read Revelation 4:1. After receiving messages for the seven churches, what did John see? What kind of voice did John hear? What did the voice John heard say to him?

2. What is the big thing that is missing in the Old Testament? Hint: This missing element makes it difficult to distinguish between first coming and the Second Coming of Christ storylines in Old Testament prophecies.

3. Read Ephesians 3:2-11. In verse 3, Paul spoke of the "mystery" that God revealed to him. What is the mystery? Why do you think Paul describes it as, "this grace," that was given to Paul in verse 8? What was God's purpose keeping this mystery hidden during the Old Testament times (verses 10–11)?

4. Read 2 Samuel 7:8–16. What specific promises did God make to David? Who is the offspring who will build a house for the Lord and whose kingdom God will establish? How does verse 14b fit as a description of Jesus? How long did God promise to establish the throne of David?

5. What are the differences between the pre-tribulation, mid-tribulation, pre-wrath, and post-tribulation views concerning the Rapture? What is your view and why?

Chapter 6: The Gospel of the Kingdom

1. Compare Mark 1:14–15 and Acts 20:24. Explain the difference between the gospel that Jesus preached (the Gospel of the Kingdom) and the gospel that we preach today (the Gospel of Grace). What gospel will be proclaimed during the Tribulation (see Matthew 24:14)?

2. Read Matthew 4:17-25. Notice that Jesus's message in verse 17 is identical to John the Baptist's message in Matthew 3:2. Why is this significant? What is Matthew trying to show?

3. How does Jesus demonstrate His message, "The kingdom of heaven is near/at hand," in this passage? How does knowing, "the kingdom of heaven is near/at hand," help us to put into context and understand the Sermon on the Mount (Matthew 5–7)?

4. Read Romans 14:10c–12 and 2 Corinthians 5:10. If we are saved by grace through faith, how is it possible for Christians to be judged, "so that each of us may receive what is due us for the things done while in the body, whether good or bad?" What will each person do when standing before God's Judgment Seat?

5. Read 1 Corinthians 3:10–15. What does it mean to be careful how one builds? How will the quality of our work be revealed on the day of judgment? Summarize the point Paul is making in this passage.

SECTION 3
THE OLIVET DISCOURSE

Chapter 7: Setting the Scene

1. In your opinion, why do so many people desire to know the date and time of Jesus's return? Why do you think those who make a prediction—publicly or otherwise, claiming it's prophetic— totally ignore passages warning against doing so?

2. Browse through Matthew 23:13–29. What words would you use to describe the teachers of the law and the Pharisees? Why do you think it was necessary to condemn the religious leaders before the whole community?

3. Read Matthew 23:29–39. How did Jesus argue that the Pharisees had failed to learn the lessons of Israel's history? Because of Jerusalem's awful leadership, how did Jesus lament over the city?

4. Read Matthew 24:1–3. Both the Temple's size and symbolism gave the Israelites a sense of security. When Jesus told the disciples the Temple would be destroyed, how do you think they felt? Following this, the disciples asked two questions. Put those two questions into your own words.

5. The disciples asked, "When?" in Matthew 24:3. Scan through the next few paragraphs. Why do you think Jesus did not answer them more directly?

Chapter 8: Events during the Tribulation

1. What kind of image does a typical politician try to project when running for office? How have you found this image to be different from what the person is really like?

2. Read Matthew 24:4-14. Jesus taught that this time would be very unstable. What signs of instability does He mention? How are these signs like, "the beginning of birth pains?" In this context, what do birth pains lead to, the Rapture or the actual Second Coming of Christ? Remember, the Church Age is not in view in Matthew 24.

3. What will happen to believers, both genuine and false, as the end approaches? What will it mean for believers to "stand firm" during these times?

4. Read Matthew 24:15–26. When the, "abomination that causes desolation," comes, what actions would believers need to take and why? Jesus describes a time of unparalleled disaster. How did He instruct people to react to it? What promise is given in verse 22?

5. According to verse 14, what must happen before the end comes? How is this message similar to what Jesus and John the Baptist preached (see Matthew 3:2; 4:17, 23)? Is this the message we are proclaiming today, in the Church Age? If not, what message are we proclaiming today (see Acts 20:24)?

Chapter 9: The End of the Tribulation

1. Read Matthew 24:27–31. As Jesus followers watch for His return during those days, how will they be able to tell the difference between false Christs and the One true Christ?

2. Read Matthew 24:36–42. Does the event described in verses 40–41 refer to the Rapture of the Church or to something else? What clue do you find in verse 37 to help you answer the question? Hoes does Luke 17:34–37 give us further clarification as to what is happening with this event?

3. Read Matthew 25:14–30. A talent was a vast sum of money. In the parable of the talents, what was the master's expectations of his servants? How does the master demonstrate his approval or disapproval? What resources and responsibilities has Jesus given you? How can you handle them in a good and faithful manner?

4. Read Matthew 25:31–46. On what basis are the sheep and the goats separated? What does the surprise of the righteous (the sheep) indicate about the possible motives for the good works they did? What does the defense of the unrighteous (the goats) indicate about the lack of their faith?

5. Scan through the three parables of Matthew 25. Even though these parables don't apply directly to Church Age saints, what points of application can we still glean as we await the Rapture of the Church?

SECTION 4
FROM THE PERSPECTIVE OF REVELATION

Chapter 10: Blockbuster at the Movie Theater

1. Scan Revelation 5 and 6. How do Revelation 5 and 6 picture the
    two theater screens concept presented in chapter 10 of this book?
    How does seeing the text of prophecy unfold in Revelation 6
    make you feel?

2. Read Revelation 5:1–14. For what is the Lamb praised and
    worshipped (verses 9–13)? How has the Lamb triumphed (verse
    5)? How has the Lamb purchased men for God with His blood
    (verse 9)? Why do you think the Lamb's triumph makes Him
    worthy to open the seals on the scroll?

3. Read Revelation 6:9–17. How does the experience of the
    believers (verses 9–11) contrast with those of the unbelievers
    (verses 15–17) as they anticipate the impending wrath of God?
    What evidence, if any, do you see of this contrast among people
    in our world today?

4. Read Revelation 7:1–4, 9–14. There are two groups of people identified in chapters 6 and 7: those who do not belong to God (Revelation 6:15–17) and those who do belong to Him (Revelation 7). What is the difference in their reactions to everything that God has been doing?

5. Listen to the message of the fifth angel in Revelation 7:2–3. What does it mean to be sealed? Who benefits from the process? How is this seal different from the mark in Revelation 13:16–17?

Chapter 11: "Let's Go Surfing Now, Everybody's Learning How"

1. Do you have a grasp of the wave concept in understanding the timeline of Revelation as presented in chapter 11 of this book? Try to explain the wave concept in your own words.

2. Read Revelation 6:12–17. This passage details the sixth seal. It seems as if we are at the end of the Tribulation in these moments, but we're only in chapter 6 of Revelation. How does that fit the idea of the waves crashing into shore and then receding (see the third paragraph of chapter 11 of this book)?

3. Read Revelation 9:20–21. How will people respond to the first six trumpet-plagues? How will three and a half years of testimony from the two witnesses affect these people (see Revelation 11:3–12)? What encouragement for Christians does the story of the two witnesses offer even now?

4. Read Revelation 11:15–19. With the blowing of the seventh trumpet comes a heavenly chorus of joy. What do you think this signifies? Why is Heaven singing when we still have six chapters before John describes the return of Christ?

5. Read Revelation 17:1–4 and 18:1–3. Why is Babylon described as an adulteress or prostitute? How does false religion (Revelation 17) or materialism (Revelation 18) seduce?

Chapter 12: Don't Forget the Main Thing

1. As you consider the subject of God's wrath, what thoughts and feelings do you have? Explain.

2. Read Revelation 16:1-11. The scene here describes the end of the Tribulation, just before Christ's return. Summarize the events during the first five seals.

3. Read Revelation 16:12–21. Note the similarity between the plagues of Revelation 16 and those brought on Egypt (blood, frogs, gnats, flies, livestock, boils, hail, locusts, darkness, firstborn (Exodus 7–12). What might be meant by this comparison?

4. How could the same events lead to worship on the parts of some (Revelation 16:5–7) and cursing on the part of others (Revelation 16:9, 21)?

5. If we realize that the wrath of God will one day be fully expressed, what difference should it make in our attitudes toward sin? In our attitudes toward unjust suffering? In our attitudes toward non-Christians?

SECTION 5
THE END OF THE STORY

Chapter 13: The Actual Return and the Kingdom

1. Explain the difference between all the events leading up to and including the Second Coming of Christ and just the actual event of the Second Coming of Christ (refer to the beginning of chapter 13 in this book).

2. Read Revelation 19:11–21. Like a champion ready for battle, Jesus appears. What do we learn about Him here? What do all the symbols tell you about Him? How does this snapshot of Christ compare to the typical image most people have of Him?

3. Would you describe the final battle described in Revelation 19 as anticlimactic? Why or why not?

4. Read Revelation 20:1-4. The thousand-year reign of Christ (Millennium) has been interpreted as referring to: (a) a period of righteousness and peace on earth before Christ's return (postmillennial), (b) Christ's reign in Heaven between His first coming and Second Comings (millennial), and (c) Christ's reign on earth after His return (premillennial). Which view do you think best fits this passage and the book of Revelation?

5. Read Revelation 20:4–6. How might this passage be an answer to the believer's prayer, "Your kingdom come … on earth as it is in heaven"? How can this passage help us to see life and death in proper perspective?

Chapter 14: The Great White Throne and the Eternal State

1. When you were a kid, what did you think Heaven would be like? What are you most looking forward to about Heaven and why?

2. Read Revelation 20:7–10. What is the nature and outcome of Satan's last outing? Why do you think God allows Satan to be paroled for this brief season?

3. Read Revelation 20:11–15. Who will be judged at the great white throne judgment? Who will be judged, and who will not be judged here? On what basis will the people be judged? What does it say about God's character that He would keep a record of what each person had done in their lifetimes?

4. Read Revelation 21:1–8. Our eternal home is described both as a city and a bride, pictures that speak to our longings for community and intimacy. What is it about living forever in close community with others that sounds appealing to you? How do you think marriage reflects the kind of intimacy we will experience in Heaven? According to verse 3, Heaven isn't primarily about a place, but about a person. Why is it that God is the only one who can captivate our innermost longings?

5. What is the difference between the first death and the second death? What about the first and second resurrections? What does the future hold for all of those who follow Christ?

Chapter 15: How Should We Respond?

1. What is there in your life that would cause you to say, "Hold on, I'm not yet ready for this life to be over"? What makes you uneasy about the return of Jesus Christ?

2. Read Revelation 22:6-21. What ideas are repeated in verses 7, 10, 12, and 20? What implications do these truths have for your life and in your response to the study of the End Times?

3. How do you respond to the first application point of chapter 15 in this book: We should make plans as if Jesus isn't coming back for a thousand years? Are there any plans you need to make or adjust as you consider the remainder of your life?

4. How do you respond to the second application point of chapter 15 in this book: At the same time, you live your life as if Jesus could return at any moment? How should you prepare for the fact that the Rapture of the Church is imminent—it could happen at any moment?

5. How do you respond to the third application point of chapter 15 in this book: Ask and answer yourself this question, "Am I in the faith?" Have you followed the prescription found in 2 Corinthians 13:5–6? What was the outcome?

ABOUT THE AUTHOR

Rich Chasse has been the teaching pastor at CrossRoads Church of Mason County, Michigan, for the past twenty-two years. He is also the host and teacher on the Bible study podcast *Daily in the Word with Rich Chasse,* which is available on most major podcast platforms or at the website, DailyInTheWord.info. For more information or to inquire about speaking engagements, please contact via email at: richchasse@yahoo.com. Rich and his wife, Sherie, have three grown children and four grandchildren, and reside in Scottville, Michigan.

Printed in the United States
by Baker & Taylor Publisher Services